Contents

Introduction

LGBT+ Issues is Volume 369 in the **ISSUES** series. The aim of the series is to offer current, diverse information about important issues in our world, from a UK perspective.

ABOUT LGBT+ ISSUES

With one in five young people identifying as LGBT+, gender identity and sexuality is an increasingly important topic. To help readers understand gender and sexuality, this book looks at and explores the issues that face young people today, such as legal rights, mental health and LGBT+ awareness.

OUR SOURCES

Titles in the **ISSUES** series are designed to function as educational resource books, providing a balanced overview of a specific subject.

The information in our books is comprised of facts, articles and opinions from many different sources, including:

- ◆ Newspaper reports and opinion pieces
- ◆ Website factsheets
- ◆ Magazine and journal articles
- ◆ Statistics and surveys
- ◆ Government reports
- ◆ Literature from special interest groups.

A NOTE ON CRITICAL EVALUATION

Because the information reprinted here is from a number of different sources, readers should bear in mind the origin of the text and whether the source is likely to have a particular bias when presenting information (or when conducting their research). It is hoped that, as you read about the many aspects of the issues explored in this book, you will critically evaluate the information presented.

It is important that you decide whether you are being presented with facts or opinions. Does the writer give a biased or unbiased report? If an opinion is being expressed, do you agree with the writer? Is there potential bias to the 'facts' or statistics behind an article?

ASSIGNMENTS

In the back of this book, you will find a selection of assignments designed to help you engage with the articles you have been reading and to explore your own opinions. Some tasks will take longer than others and there is a mixture of design, writing and research-based activities that you can complete alone or in a group.

FURTHER RESEARCH

At the end of each article we have listed its source and a website that you can visit if you would like to conduct your own research. Please remember to critically evaluate any sources that you consult and consider whether the information you are viewing is accurate and unbiased.

Useful Websites

www.amnesty.org.uk

www.childandfamilyblog.com

www.counselling-directory.org.uk

www.euronews.com

www.fullfact.org

www.fumble.org.uk

www.independent.co.uk

www.inews.co.uk

www.medicalnewstoday.com

www.mentalhealth.org.uk

www.ons.gov.uk

www.outlife.org.uk

www.stonewall.org.uk

www.telegraph.co.uk

www.theguardian.com

www.unherd.com

www.uniteuk1.com

www.worldatlas.com

www.yougov.co.uk

MWA1

Please return/renew this item by the last
date shown. Books may also be renewed
by phone or internet.

💻 www.rbwm.gov.uk/home/leisure-and-
culture/libraries

☎ 01628 796969 (library hours)

☎ 0303 123 0035 (24 hours)

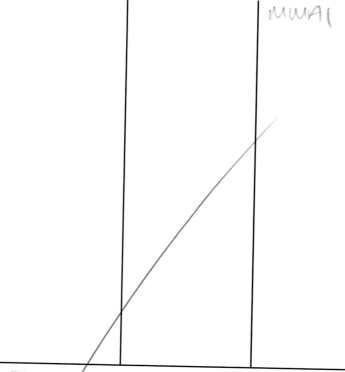

Independence Educational Publishers

First published by Independence Educational Publishers

The Studio, High Green

Great Shelford

Cambridge CB22 5EG

England

ISBN-13: 978 1 86168 826 2

Printed in Great Britain

Zenith Print Group

What's the difference between sex and gender?

Sex and gender identity can be a complicated subject. Here is our (very) basic introduction to the difference between sex and gender.

Have you ever wondered about the difference between sex and gender? They're two very different things, but people often get them mixed up or find them confusing. There are lots of different terms that relate to sex and gender, but this article is about an easy-to-understand introduction to this complex question.

What is sex?

For once, we're not talking about intercourse. When you were born, a doctor or a nurse will have assigned you a 'sex' by examining which biological reproductive organs you have, what sex chromosomes are inside your body, or even by measuring your hormone levels. These sexes are:

Male – The sex assigned to a boy or man who produces sperm cells via the testes. They have an XY sex chromosome, and often higher levels of the testosterone hormone.

Female – The sex assigned to a girl or woman who produces egg cells via the ovaries, which make up part of the female reproductive system. They have breasts, an XX sex chromosome, and often higher levels of the oestrogen hormone.

Intersex or DSD (Differences in Sex Development) – Terms used to describe the variations that can occur in chromosomes, genitals or internal reproductive organs. A person may present with a DSD at birth, puberty or later in life.

What is gender?

Once you've been assigned a sex at birth, everything from the clothes you wear, to the hair on your head, the way you behave, and the activities you engage in, will all play a part in shaping the gender you identify as.

It's very important to remember that your gender is not the same as your sex. Gender is personally unique to you, and is not determined by your reproductive organs.

People identify with gender in a way that is personal and unique to them, and not everyone has a gender identity. Some people have a very strong gender identity, some don't identify with any gender at all, others see their gender as fluid, it all depends on who you are. There is no one right or wrong way to identify with gender.

What are the different types of gender?

There are a variety of terms that people use to identify their gender, which include:

Cisgender – Cisgender is a term used to describe someone whose sex they were given at birth matches the gender they identify themselves as. For example; I was assigned the sex of male, I was born with a penis, and I identify as a male. Therefore, I am Cisgender.

Transgender – Transgender (or trans for short) is a term used to address someone whose gender identity is different from the sex they were assigned to at birth. For example; I was assigned the sex female at birth, I have a vagina and breasts, but I identify as a male. Therefore, I am Transgender.

Genderqueer – A term used which address someone who identifies themselves as a gender that falls outside of the 'male' or 'female' restrictions. For example; I was assigned the sex of male at birth, I have a penis, but I identify myself as both male and female. Therefore I am Genderqueer. However, other Genderqueer people may choose to identify themselves as having no gender at all.

Gender is not just about being one way or the other – it's a very complex spectrum. So, while we hope this post has helped clear a few things up, don't worry if you're still feeling confused.

And remember, the most important thing when talking about sex and gender is to always be respectful of a person's personal gender identity.

The Fumble Glossary of Gender and Sexuality

An introductory list of terms relating to sexuality and gender

Gender and sexuality can be confusing at first. Never fear, however – Fumble is here.

Below is a list of some of the key terms you might come across.

Gender

Agender: literally translates as 'without gender'. It can mean not having a binary gender, or not having any gender identity at all.

Biological sex: a label given at birth based on medical factors (including chromosomes, genitals and hormones).

Cisgender: a person whose biological sex and gender identity align.

Gender: social structures (e.g. rights, social roles) largely based on cultural norms, and assumed from biological sex. Gender can be considered different from sex, which is assigned and based on primary sex characteristics (e.g. genitalia).

Gender binary: the splitting of gender into two distinct sets – male (masculine) and female (feminine).

Gender expression: how someone chooses to express their gender identity (e.g. through clothing).

Gender identity: an individual's personal experience of their own gender.

Gender pronouns: the word(s) a person uses to refer to themselves based on their gender e.g. 'she/her', 'he/him', 'they/them'. Different people are comfortable with different words.

Gender variant: (can include terms such as genderfluid, agender, genderqueer) – a person who doesn't always define themselves within the gender binary of male/female.

Non-binary: a broad term for people who don't fit within the gender binary. For example, people may not identify as either male or female, or may identify as both.

Transgender (trans): a broad term to describe people whose gender identity doesn't align with the sex they were assigned at birth.

Transgender man: someone who has been assigned female at birth but identifies as a male. Sometimes this can be shortened to trans man or FTM ('female-to-male').

Transgender woman: someone who was assigned male at birth, but identifies as a woman. Sometimes this can be shortened to trans woman or MTF ('male-to-female').

Transitioning: the process a trans person undertakes to live in the gender they identify as. Each person's process is unique, and can comprise a combination of different steps. Some trans people have medical intervention to change their gender, and some don't.

Transsexual: an older term for people who have transitioned from their assigned gender to their preferred gender identity. Some people still identify as transsexual, whilst others do not.

Sexuality

Asexual: someone who experiences no – or little – sexual attraction.

Bisexual: someone who is attracted to two genders (often male/female or their own gender/other genders).

Demisexual: someone who is only sexually attracted to people with whom they have an emotional bond.

Heterosexual: someone who is attracted to those of the opposite gender.

Homosexual: someone who is attracted to people of the same gender. 'Lesbian' refers to homosexual women. 'Gay' refers to homosexual men, but can also be an umbrella term applied to homosexual women as well.

LGBTQ+: stands for 'lesbian, gay, bi, trans, queer +'. Often used as an inclusive term for anyone who identifies as non-heterosexual or non-cisgender.

Pansexual: someone who is attracted to people of any gender.

Sexuality/Sexual orientation: who a person is sexually attracted to based on their gender.

Queer: an inclusive term for people who are part of a sexuality or gender minority. In the past, 'queer' was used as a slur and isn't an identifier everyone feels comfortable with.

It's important for all of us to be recognise that gender and sexuality are deeply personal. No one has the right to determine whether how someone else identifies is valid. And if you haven't found a term on the list that you think fits, it doesn't mean there's anything wrong with you. Sexuality and gender exist on a spectrum – you might just take a little longer to find where exactly you sit on that spectrum!

Fumble (fumble.org.uk) is a digital media platform for young people to learn about sex, sexual health, their bodies, relationships, friendships, mental health, and sexuality. Our content is by young people, for young people. It's diverse, accessible and inclusive.

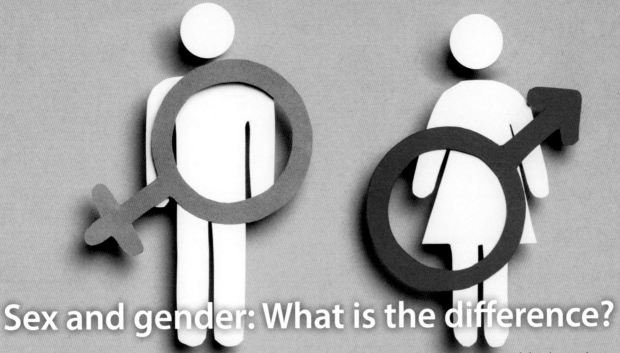

Sex and gender: What is the difference?

Historically, the terms 'sex' and 'gender' have been used interchangeably, but their uses are becoming increasingly distinct, and it is important to understand the differences between the two.

By Tim Newman

This article will look at the meaning of 'sex' and the differences between the sexes. It will also look at the meaning of 'gender,' and the concepts of gender roles, gender identity, and gender expression.

In general terms, 'sex' refers to the biological differences between males and females, such as the genitalia and genetic differences.

'Gender' is more difficult to define, but it can refer to the role of a male or female in society, known as a gender role, or an individual's concept of themselves, or gender identity.

Sometimes, a person's genetically assigned sex does not line up with their gender identity. These individuals might refer to themselves as transgender, non-binary, or gender-nonconforming.

Sex

'Sex' generally refers to biological differences.

The differences between male and female sexes are anatomical and physiological. 'Sex' tends to relate to biological differences.

For instance, male and female genitalia, both internal and external, are different. Similarly, the levels and types of hormones present in male and female bodies are different.

Genetic factors define the sex of an individual. Women have 46 chromosomes including two Xs and men have 46 including an X and a Y. The Y chromosome is dominant and carries the signal for the embryo to begin growing testes.

Both men and women have testosterone, estrogen, and progesterone. However, women have higher levels of estrogen and progesterone, and men have higher levels of testosterone.

The male/female split is often seen as binary, but this is not entirely true. For instance, some men are born with two or three X chromosomes, just as some women are born with a Y chromosome.

These cases are termed DSDs (Differences in Sex Development) or 'Intersex' and account for around 1 in 1,500 births.

Some people believe that sex should be considered a continuum rather than two mutually exclusive categories.

Gender

Gender roles vary greatly between societies.

Gender tends to denote the social and cultural role of each sex within a given society. Rather than being purely assigned by genetics, as sex differences generally are, people often develop their gender roles in response to their environment, including family interactions, the media, peers, and education.

The World Health Organization (WHO) defines gender as:

'Gender refers to the socially constructed characteristics of women and men, such as norms, roles, and relationships of and between groups of women and men. It varies from society to society and can be changed.'

Gender roles in some societies are more rigid than those in others.

The degree of decision-making and financial responsibility expected of each gender and the time that women or men are expected to spend on homemaking and rearing children varies between cultures. Within the wider culture, families too have their norms.

Gender roles are not set in stone.

In many societies, men are increasingly taking on roles traditionally seen as belonging to women, and women are playing the parts previously assigned mostly to men.

Gender roles and gender stereotypes are highly fluid and can shift substantially over time.

Who wears the high heels?

For instance, high-heeled shoes, now considered feminine throughout much of the world, were initially designed for upper-class men to use when hunting on horseback.

As women began wearing high heels, male heels slowly became shorter and fatter as female heels grew taller and thinner.

Over time, the perception of the high heel gradually became seen as feminine. There is nothing intrinsically feminine about the high heel. Social norms have made it so.

Pink for a girl and blue for a boy?

In many countries, pink is seen as a suitable colour for a girl to wear, while boys are dressed in blue.

However, infants were dressed in white until colored garments for babies were introduced in the middle of the 19th century.

The following quote comes from a trade publication called *Earnshaw's Infants' Department*, published in 1918:

'The generally accepted rule is pink for the boys and blue for the girls. The reason is that pink, being a more decided and stronger color, is more suitable for the boy, while blue, which is more delicate and dainty, is prettier for the girl.'

Move forward 100 years and it is rare to find a baby boy dressed in pink in many countries.

Identity and expression

Another meaning of gender is an individual's view of themselves, or their gender identity.

GLAAD (formerly the Gay & Lesbian Alliance Against Defamation) describes gender identity as:

'One's internal, personal sense of being a man or woman. For transgender people, their own internal gender identity does not match the sex they were assigned at birth.

Most people have a gender identity of man or woman (or boy or girl). For some people, their gender identity does not fit neatly into one of those two choices.'

Similarly, GLAAD describes gender expression as follows:

'External manifestations of gender, expressed through one's name, pronouns, clothing, haircut, behavior, voice, or body characteristics. Society identifies these cues as masculine and feminine, although what is considered masculine and feminine changes over time and varies by culture.'

To conclude, in general terms, 'sex' refers to biological characteristics and 'gender' refers to the individual's and society's perceptions of sexuality and the malleable concepts of masculinity and femininity.

7 February 2018

Sex stereotypes and the development of gender identity disorder in children

By Dr Katie Alcock, Chartered Psychologist, Senior Lecturer in Psychology at Lancaster University

Sex stereotypes and the impact on children

We know that boys and girls are treated differently from the moment the baby's sex is confirmed – these days before birth. We have known for decades that behaviour towards an infant depends on whether an adult is told the infant is a boy or a girl but in recent years the possibility of finding out a baby's sex before birth has extended the exposure of infants to stereotyped talk and behaviour to their time in the womb, even by women's studies researchers – insidiously, this includes allocation of family resources in some societies.

And boys' and girls' worlds are very different, even in the first few years of life.

Children rapidly come to understand that there are two classes of humans – boys and girls. The stereotypes they absorb in relation to each sex are affected by family and society.

What do children understand about the existence of two sexes and when?

Research has long shown that children move through a series of stages in their understanding of who is a boy and who is a girl and how this develops. Kohlberg noted that children first work out that they, themselves, are a boy or a girl, in a process very similar to learning what animals are cats versus dogs – **by using perceptual features**. In other words, children categorise boys and girls (including themselves) by their stereotyped appearances and behaviours. This early identification happens around 18 months to 3 years and is known as 'sex identity' or (in more recent literature) 'gender identity'. The psychological literature around the development of this concept, until very recently, referred only to children's knowledge of their own biological sex; and it is not a complex concept like some adults feel about their own identity, it relies on the same processes children use to work out what is a table versus a chair or a car versus a bus. Children identify other children solely on the basis of the other children's dress and toy preferences. This is not too surprising given the sex-stereotype saturated world they have grown up in.

Following this early identification of one's own sex, children come to realise that they cannot change sex. Prior to this, they think that even though they are a girl, they can grow up to be a man, have a beard and inseminate a woman (e.g. put a seed in a Mummy's tummy); boys think they can grow up to be a woman, have breasts and be pregnant and breastfeed. Children believe that changing appearance, accessories and toys leads an individual to change sex, immediately.

Children believe that changing appearance, accessories and toys leads an individual to change sex, immediately.

Once they have learned that they themselves cannot change sex (sex or gender stability), children are still uncertain – **in some cases up to the age of 9** – about whether other people can change sex. S. L. Bem discovered that one of the important features in children realising that sex is constant is children's knowledge of the genitals of each sex. There is also a clear link to another important milestone in children's cognitive development – the understanding of the appearance-reality distinction. Children who have not yet reached this phase of understanding will believe that a cat that puts on a dog mask has really and truly turned into a dog. We now know that children who understand that sex cannot change – who have reached the gender/sex constancy phase – must have both the understanding that appearance does not change reality, AND the understanding that boys have one set of genitals and girls another.

This all explains very well how children in toddler years are susceptible to sex stereotypes, with a peak in preschool and early school age years, and how they become more flexible around stereotypes around the age of 7-8+. It is important for children, in order not to fall into traps (which can be lifelong traps) about their own and others' capabilities falling along stereotyped lines, to understand the reality of sex and of stereotyping early.

The consequences of diagnosing children with gender identity disorder based on sex stereotypes.

Much of the research I have cited here was carried out in an era when, like Bussey and Bandura, people felt that gender was 'one of the most important ways of categorising people'. We would hope that it's possible for parents to move beyond this feeling that they need to know what their child's gendered behaviour is going to be like; however it is with this background that the diagnostic criteria for gender identity disorder in childhood were set. In order for a child to be diagnosed with gender identity disorder, they must adhere to sex-typed stereotypes of the opposite sex – they must meet six criteria from a set of nine – of these, five refer to play and dress that is stereo-typically associated with the opposite sex, including playing with the opposite sex.

In order for a child to be diagnosed with gender identity disorder, they must adhere to sex-typed stereotypes of the opposite sex.

But we no longer wish to live in that world. We do not want our children to think that some things are only for boys and some for girls. Believing this holds women back. If we lived in a world where no toys or dress or behaviour was stereotyped, it would not be possible for children to be diagnosed with gender dysphoria; in fact, one would hope that children would be happier in their sexed bodies if they had no indication that their preferred toys and games were 'supposed to be' for the opposite sex.

Additionally, children also believe that gender preferences are essential – part of children's own selves – and that they would develop in the absence of role models for that sex that adhere to stereotypes. This would imply that it is particularly difficult to counter children's ideas about sex stereotyping – which we also know from previous research on children's lack of understanding of sex constancy.

Children also believe that gender preferences are essential – part of children's own selves.

We know however that biological sex cannot change in humans (despite niche theories that it can); it's not possible to do medical or biological research with humans and believe that it can.

However, **some groups of children are delayed in this understanding** – children who transition to present as the opposite sex (socially, in other words with no hormone treatments) and their siblings believe for longer that sex can change. This tells us that children exposed to the idea that sex is not constant (their sibling who was previously a boy is now a girl, which they have found out at an age when they do not yet understand that biological sex is immutable) are then delayed in this biological understanding, long understood to be a basic developmental process.

Children are also less accepting towards children who are transgender and have transitioned socially; this is not too surprising as children are also less accepting of gender-non-conforming but non-transitioned children. We could counter this by telling children that it is fine to be gender-non-conforming, but the message that they have from all around is that girls wear pink and play with dolls, boys wear blue and play with trucks. This non-accepting behaviour is a very strong argument for teaching children that all children, boys and girls, can wear all types of clothes and play with all types of toys – not that it is OK for a few boys to wear pink, but that ALL boys can wear pink, and (importantly for the way in which children develop stereotypes) making sure that we influence society so that all boys DO wear pink.

Most children with gender dysphoria are comfortable in their birth sex by adulthood. Our aim should be to make children more comfortable as children (and making their environment less sexist would help this) so they can ease into puberty – and as a side effect their peers will accept their gender-non-conforming behaviour more if there is less gender stereotyping in general.

2 March 2020

Gender dysphoria

Gender dysphoria, also known as gender identity disorder (GID) is when a person is born one gender, but is unhappy living that way.

There are lots of children and young people who feel that their gender identity is not a complete match with the sex they were assigned at birth. Imagine your sense of self not matching your physical being - feeling this way can be very distressing. While gender dysphoria is not a mental health problem, it can cause the person a great deal of stress.

Hiding your true identity, along with growing up in a society filled with misunderstanding and stigma, will undoubtedly affect you.

What is gender dysphoria?

Gender dysphoria, or gender identity disorder, is when someone is born one gender, but identifies as another. This may mean that a person born a male identifies as female, or vice versa.

Some people may not identify with a gender at all.

People who feel this way are most commonly known as 'transgender' or 'trans'; however, we understand that trans people self-identify in many ways. Throughout this fact-sheet, we will use 'trans' as an inclusive term, which embraces trans, transgender, gender nonconforming and gender variant, among others.

Non-binary gender identity

People can also describe themselves as 'non-binary', which is when they do not feel they are male nor female. Non-binary also embraces those who identify as androgyne, thirdgender and polygender, who are not comfortable thinking of themselves as simply male or female. They may identify as a combination of the two, or neither.

Signs of gender dysphoria

It's common for the signs of gender dysphoria to show at a very early age. Children may refuse to wear certain clothes or dislike taking part in typical boys or girls' activities. Other behaviours may include:

- insisting that they are of the opposite sex

- wanting to wear clothes typically worn by the other sex, and disliking or refusing to wear clothes typically worn by their sex

- wanting to take part in and play with members of the opposite sex, while refusing to take part in activities typically with and for their sex

- insisting or hoping that their genitals will change

- feeling extreme distress at puberty and the physical changes that will occur

- feelings of anxiety and depression

In many cases, these behaviours are just a part of the child growing up. Yet if the feelings of gender dysphoria are still present as they go through their teenage years and into adulthood, it is likely that it is not a stage of development, and further support may be needed.

While many people with gender dysphoria will feel this way during early childhood, this isn't always the case. Some people may not recognise their feelings for what they are until adulthood, or they simply learn to suppress and hide the feelings to avoid peer and family rejection while growing up.

Puberty forces changes on a body that can feel particularly uncomfortable. Unwanted changes are happening, so while a child may have enjoyed being androgynous growing up, the secondary sex characteristics of puberty can be very distressing.

There are no physical signs of gender dysphoria, but there are specific behaviours that people may display.

If you are a teenager or adult, whose feelings of gender dysphoria started in childhood, you may now feel like you have a much clearer sense of your identity and how you want to deal with it. You may be certain that your gender identity is at odds with your assigned sex, a strong desire to hide or be rid of the physical signs of your sex, such as breasts and body hair.

> 'A strong, resonate thought that shook me to the core: I don't want to be a girl anymore.' Zach

How will I know if I have it?

Only you can ever say how you feel. Some people will know from a very young age, while others will feel like they don't 'fit' with members of their sex, but not know what to do, or how to tell people how they feel. Many people will keep their thoughts and feelings to themselves, living a life in a body they aren't happy in.

Everyone deserves to live the life they want. This is why we are passionate about raising awareness of issues and providing people with the information and support they need.

The Equality Act 2010

Gender reassignment is a protected characteristic under the Equality Act 2010. This means you are protected by law if you are a victim harassment or discrimination in the workplace, and wider society.

Living with gender dysphoria

It can be very distressing, keeping how you feel to yourself. Whether through lack of support or information or from fear of judgement or discrimination, living a life where you are unhappy, really, is no life at all.

Gender dysphoria is not a mental illness, however, people who experience gender dysphoria often suffer great stress as a result of hiding their identity. This is why it is so important that we speak about these issues - society needs to understand and be more aware of the issues and feelings many people experience. Talking about it and supporting each other is the first step to breaking down the stigma, and helping trans people feel more comfortable in reaching out and asking for help. Nobody should feel they have to keep quiet about who they are.

'According to charity Stonewall, two in five trans people (41%) said that when accessing general health care services in 2017, healthcare staff lacked understanding of trans health needs.'

'I was fortunate enough to have a mother and sister who were more understanding than I could have dreamt. Even though it upset them that they were losing a daughter and sister, they were happy to see the confident, care-free young man I was becoming.'

If a person has made the decision to change their gender role, this is known as 'transition'. This enables them to express themselves in line with their gender identity, perhaps by choosing a new name and changing their appearance, like changing their hair or wearing different clothes. The way in which individuals express themselves will vary from person to person, everyone is different and these changes take time.

Coming out as transgender

Telling people about your sexuality or gender identity is called 'coming out'. Coming out is an incredibly individual process and it's not necessarily a one-off event. Lesbian, gay, bi and trans people may have to come out many times during their lives and sadly, many people will face a number of challenges when doing so.

How you come out will depend on you and what you feel comfortable with. For example, you may feel comfortable speaking about your gender identity with your close friends, but not with your family. Remember, coming out may be difficult and takes an immense amount of courage.

If you have decided that you are ready to tell people, it can help to sit and really think about how you want to tell them. Consider where and how you tell them. Depending on who you talk to, they may have questions, so be prepared to answer them, or tell them if you're not ready.

If they react badly, remember that they may just need some time to absorb what you've told them. While you can't predict how people will respond, if you have told a close friend you trust, the chances are they'll be pleased you've shared something so personal and support you.

Don't feel under pressure to come out - take your time. Only you will know when you're ready to talk and asking for help isn't easy. If you feel ready to come out, but are unsure of how to broach the subject with loved ones, visit Stonewall for more information.

The next steps

Treatment for gender dysphoria aims to help people live the way they want to, as the gender they identify with. What this means will vary for each person, and is different for children, young people and adults.

The first step is to speak to a professional. Whether this is your GP, or a psychotherapist or counsellor, if you have come to the decision that you want further treatment, professional support is essential.

Children and young people

Under 18s will typically be referred to a specialist child and adolescent Gender Identity Clinic (GIC), where staff will carry out a detailed assessment, to help determine what support they need. Treatment will vary depending on the results of the assessment and the age of the child, though options include:

◆ family therapy

◆ individual child psychotherapy

◆ parental support or counselling

◆ regular reviews

◆ hormone therapy

Also, know that schools have a legal duty to support trans students (even single-sex schools) and many are doing so very well. If you or your child is at school and would like support outside of a professional environment, consider speaking to the student support services if available, or your teacher. They will be able to explain the support available and together you can decide on the next steps.

Adults

Adults with gender dysphoria should be referred to a specialist adult GIC. As with children and young people, these clinics can offer ongoing support and advice, assessments and treatment. This may include:

◆ mental health support, such as counselling

◆ cross-sex hormone treatment

◆ speech and language therapy

◆ peer support groups

Some people find that the support and advice from a specialist clinic is all they need to feel comfortable in their transition. Others will need more extensive treatment, such as a full transition to the opposite sex. The level of treatment you receive is completely down to you - only you know what you need and how you feel.

Hormone therapy

Hormone therapy is prescribed to help make individuals more comfortable with themselves - in terms of both physical appearance, and how they feel. If undergoing hormone therapy, individuals will take the hormone of their preferred gender. Whether testosterone or oestrogen, the hormones will start the process of changing the body into one that is more male or female.

Typically, this will be a lifelong treatment, even if you have had genital reconstructive surgery.

'The goal I'd been striving towards for so long was now a reality, my normal.'

Social gender role transition

If you are considering a full transition and requiring surgery, you are typically required to first live in your preferred gender identity full time for at least one year. This is known as 'social gender role transition' (previously known as 'real life experience') and will help in confirming whether permanent surgery is the right option for you.

Once you have completed your social gender role transition, and you and your care team are confident you are ready, you may decide to go ahead with the surgery.

Finding support

As we said, gender dysphoria is not a mental illness. Yet, living a life that you feel isn't yours can be detrimental to your mental health and well-being. The confusion, the fear of judgement, the isolation, the stress. All of these things can affect a person's mental health and if untreated, can lead to further problems.

Talking is an incredibly helpful tool, wherever you are in your journey. Of course, this can be easier said than done, and sadly, stigma and misunderstanding is still present in today's society. If you're not ready to talk to friends and family, seeking professional support can be an option.

A counsellor experienced in gender dysphoria and trans people will have an understanding of what you are going through, and the options available to you. They can offer you a safe place to talk, free of stigma and judgement, and without shame. In the counselling room, you can be you.

Know that all counselling professional bodies have outlawed 'conversion' or 'reparative' therapies. While counsellors can offer you a safe space to explore gender dysphoria, they are not permitted to attempt to 'convert' someone's gender or sexuality.

March 2018

What does non-binary mean? Definition after Sam Smith comes out as genderqueer

The singer said he doesn't identify as male or female.

By Sarah Young

Last week, Sam Smith revealed that he identifies as non-binary and genderqueer.

During an interview with Jameela Jamil on Instagram, the British singer spoke about listening to conversations about being non-binary and realising that is how he identified.

'When I saw the word 'non-binary', 'genderqueer', and I read into it, and I heard these people speaking I was like, 'F***, that is me',' he told the presenter.

But, what exactly does it mean to be non-binary?

While Smith defined the term as a 'mixture of all different things', revealing he doesn't identify as 'male or female', non-binary can mean different things to different people.

Here, we take a look at the definition of the term, explore how it differs to being transgender and reveal what you can do to be a better ally to non-binary individuals.

What does non-binary mean?

According to Stonewall UK – a charity that campaigns for the equality of lesbian, gay, bi and trans people across Britain – non-binary is described as an 'umbrella term for people whose gender identity doesn't sit comfortably with 'man' or 'woman''.

The definition is purposefully broad given its multiple definitions.

While some non-binary individuals identify as either having a gender which is in-between the two categories 'man' and 'woman', others can fluctuate between them, or have no gender, either permanently or some of the time.

The LGBT Foundation – a charity that supports the needs of the diverse range of people who identify as lesbian, gay, bisexual and trans – explains that there are a number of other terms people within the non-binary community may also use to describe their gender, including genderqueer, neutrosis, agender, gender fluid, bigender and third gender.

Why the term non-binary?

As the National Centre for Transgender Equality explains, 'some societies – like ours – tend to recognise just two genders, male and female.'

This concept, which suggests there are only two genders, is often referred to as a gender binary, with binary meaning 'having two parts'. Therefore, 'non-binary' is a term people can use to 'describe genders that don't fall into one of these two categories, male or female'.

Is non-binary different to being transgender?

Transgender is a term used to describe people 'whose gender is not the same as, or does not sit comfortably with, the sex they were assigned at birth,' says Stonewall UK.

For example, a transgender man is a term used to describe someone who is assigned female at birth but identifies and lives as a man.

Non-binary, on the other hand, refers to someone who does not fit into rigid gender categories and is neither female nor male.

While they can identify with aspects of either gender, they can also have an identity outside the binary, which can also change and evolve over time.

What pronouns are used to describe someone who is non-binary?

Pronouns are the words that take the place of a person's name and some people feel more comfortable using certain pronouns than others.

Non-binary people can use a range of pronouns, including 'he' and 'she'.

However, they may also prefer to use gender neutral pronouns such as 'they' and 'them' to reflect that they don't identify as either male or female.

There are also various new pronouns, including xie and xir, zie and zir, and sie and hir.

If a person is non-binary, it is perfectly polite to ask them what pronouns they would like you to use, so as to avoid using the incorrect terms.

How can you be a better ally to non-binary people?

Aside from using the correct pronouns, there are many ways you can support non-binary people.

From educating yourself on the term to being an advocate for non-binary friendly policies and donating to or fundraising for LGBTQ+ charities.

There are a number of organisations currently doing life-saving work for trans and non-binary people, including The Albert Kennedy Trust, which helps with housing needs

For more information or advice about being non-binary or any issues affecting LGBT people and their families, you can visit www.stonewall.org.uk or call the charity's information service on 08000 50 20 20.

You can also contact The Albert Kennedy Trust regarding housing on 020 7831 6562

19 March 2019

Gender nonconforming children are at greater risk of victimization, particularly boys

Gender nonconforming youth are more likely to experience rejection and verbal, physical and sexual abuse from both parents and peers.

Gender nonconforming children, particularly boys, experience victimization. They are more likely to be rejected and verbally abused by their parents, and they suffer higher levels of both depression and PTSD. Men who identify as both gay and 'effeminate' report more sexual abuse in childhood. This may be related to the general low value given to 'feminine' behaviours and characteristics. Possibly as a result, boys are less likely to be gender nonconforming than girls.

Gender identity and child development

Children learn gender labels when very young, at 18 to 21 months, shaped by parental behaviour and expectations. For example, parents give girl and boy toddlers different toys, and they often expect boys to be better at crawling than girls. At two years, children can already feel atypical if they are not like others of their own gender.

Researchers at Yale and Harvard universities in the USA reviewed how victimization of gender nonconforming children influences their development. They present a 'social cognitive' approach which proposes that gender identity develops through direct influences, such as verbal messages about how boys and girls should behave, and indirect influences, such as parents modelling gender specific behaviour. A child is an interactive agent in this process of development. The process is influenced by culture: for example, non-Western or more religious men are likely to be less accepting of gender nonconforming individuals.

Two types of socialisation have been studied: in the home and among peers

Gender socialisation at home

At home, gender socialisation takes place through things like clothing, how parents praise their boys and girls and how parents use gender specific pronouns. Experimental studies have shown that adults interacting with infants introduced as a girl were more likely to give 'feminine' toys to the child, such as dolls and domestic items. If the infant is introduced as a boy, however, they are more likely to introduce 'masculine' toys, such as tools and cars, and they encourage more physical activity. Parents support things like exploration, rough-and-tumble play and dressing up differently in boys and girls, despite a lack of evidence that boys and girls are different in any domain typically associated with gender, such as crawling ability.

Parents tend to associate gender nonconformity in children with homosexuality and often discourage gender nonconforming behaviour. Discouragement of nonconformity in children as young as four years includes telling them to change their behaviour, punishing or restricting their nonconforming activities and sending

them to counselling. Such children are also at greater risk of physical, psychological and sexual abuse in the home, and of PTSD later in life.

These problems affect sexual and gender minority youth in particular—individuals who identify as lesbian, gay, bisexual, queer, or another orientation that is not heterosexual, as well as those who identify as transgender, agender, gender fluid, or another category that is not cisgender. Transgender youth are particularly exposed to negativity from their parents.

Gender socialisation among peers

When young children play among peers, their play becomes more gendered. For example, girls are less likely to play with toy cars when they are not alone. Preschool and middle-school children are more likely to befriend same-sex children with similar levels of gender-typed behaviours. Peer popularity of children is strongly related to gender conformity across childhood: there are strong social rewards for conforming.

The process of gender socialisation is visible in trends across childhood. Over time, children's attitudes about the other gender become more similar to their friends' attitudes. Children's identification with their own gender grows; at the same time, peer harassment and victimization

of nonconforming children increase. As a result, gender nonconforming behaviour falls over the school years.

This process is linked to children's cognitive development: they are increasingly able to make social comparisons between boys and girls, to develop a sense of self around gender and to imagine what others are thinking about them.

Gender nonconforming youth are more likely to experience rejection and verbal, physical and sexual abuse from peers. They are more likely to experience low self-worth, but only when they do not feel accepted by their peers. If they do feel accepted, no increased risk of low self-worth is present.

Child development risks from negative responses to gender nonconforming children

Gender nonconforming children are more likely to suffer depression and to have suicidal thoughts. They are also at greater risk of bullying others and becoming aggressive. The authors of the review describe the process according to 'minority stress theory', which encompasses both actual discrimination and the internalized response to it on the part of the victim. Such responses may include internalized homophobia, chronic vigilance about rejection and concealment of sexual orientation.

What can be done?

Family acceptance of gender nonconforming children is important. For example, a father's acceptance of nonconforming behaviour in his son protects the child from psychological distress. (No such link occurs between fathers and daughters.)

The researchers make recommendations to parents about how to support sexual and gender minority children – talking about gender nonconformity, respecting it, ensuring other family and community members do the same, finding adult role models, and welcoming the child's friends.

Action in schools to support gender nonconforming children is particularly important given the long span of strong peer influence on child development. Again, the researchers direct their recommendations to the particular case of sexual and gender minority children. They recommend that schools explicitly address sexual orientation and gender and negative reactions to gender nonconformity. Teachers need training, and gender nonconforming students need support groups. The topic should be on the school curriculum, they write, and sexual orientation should be an explicit part of anti-bullying strategies.

February 2020

What is sexuality?

Everybody has a sexuality, it is a central part of who we are. It is made up of a few different things, such as; your sex, gender identity and roles, sexual orientation, pleasure, intimacy and reproduction. People can express their sexuality in their thoughts, desires, attitudes, behaviours, practice, roles and relationships. Sexuality is influenced by different factors, like, biology, psychology, social settings, economic factors like money, culture, history, religion and spirituality or how you see yourself.

Sexual attraction

Most people have sexual desires in some way or another. This means we find other people attractive and think about them in a sexual way. Some people want to have sex with other people, whereas others are happy to just think about it. Sexuality is about how you think and feel about sex.

Healthy sexuality is about having a confident, comfortable and communicative attitude towards yourself and your sexual desires, whether you want to have sex or not.

What does sexual orientation mean?

Part of your sexuality is your sexual orientation. Sexual orientation is who you fancy, this can mean someone of a different gender or someone of the same gender. Gender is how you identify yourself, examples of gender are Male, Female, Trans, Queer. During your teenage years, you may start exploring your sexuality and sexual orientation, to find out what you're into.

You might feel unsure about your sexual orientation, or what gender you find attractive might change during your life. This is totally ok - many people are attracted to different genders or like different things sexually at different stages in their lives.

Being LGBT

LGBT stands for lesbian, gay, bisexual or transgender.

- **Lesbian** means a woman who is attracted to other women.

- **Gay** means a man who is attracted to other men, and is sometimes used to describe women who are attracted to other women too.

- **Bisexual** means a person who is attracted to more than one gender.

- **Transgender** means someone whose gender is different from the gender they were assigned at birth.

Some people know from a young age whether they are gay, lesbian or bisexual, some people find out at different points in their life, and some people change their mind multiple times during their life. It's important to remember that not everyone fits neatly into one of these categories, and some people don't identify as either LGBTQ+ or straight.

It's OK to take your time to experiment and think about what you like. The most important thing is that you feel comfortable and proud of who you are, no matter what way you identify.

Am I LGBTQ+?

If you are usually emotionally and sexually attracted to the same gender, you may be gay or lesbian. If you feel attracted to more than one gender or have relationships with more than one gender, you may be bisexual. If your gender identity and/or gender expression differs from the gender assigned to you at birth, you may be transgender.

If you are LGBTQ+, it can be difficult to tell someone and working out whether you are gay, lesbian, bisexual or straight can be a confusing time. You don't have to tell your friends anything about your sexual orientation or who you fancy unless you want to, but remember it can help to talk. These things take time and there are trusted professionals who can help you if you want to chat.

If you think you are gay, lesbian or bisexual, there's nothing wrong with exploring those feelings and having relationships to help you decide.

Many people will experience crushes on someone of the same sex as they are growing up and this can mean that they are gay or lesbian, but their feelings may also change and they can find that they are more attracted to the opposite gender, or both genders.

Coming out

Coming out is the process of accepting yourself as LGBT and being open about this with other people. Coming out can be difficult, but it can also be totally worth it.

www.outlife.org.uk

A-Z of sexual orientation

What is sexual orientation?

Sexual orientation is a term that is used to describe what gender, or genders, someone is attracted to. The most common sexual orientations that people identify with are straight, gay, lesbian or bisexual, but there's a whole pile of other terms and language around it that are important to know too. Make sure not to confuse it with gender identity - sexual orientation describes what gender or genders you're attracted to, and gender identity describes what gender or genders you are.

Please note, that although we tried to list as many terms as we can here, sexual orientation is a super complex issue, and new terms are being developed to describe different orientations and ways of thinking about sexual orientation and attraction all the time. It's always important to respect everyone's sexual orientation, even if they identify as something you've never heard of before.

Remember, sexual orientation can be fluid, and many people identify as different orientations at different stages of their lives. It's totally fine to question your sexual orientation, and to identify with something different than what you did before.

We understand also that if you feel your particular sexual orientation isn't represented or accurately described by any popular terms, you might feel pretty alienated and alone. But you should try to realise that whatever you identify with is absolutely fine and great, even if there's no popular word out there that describes it. You might just be a bit ahead of your time, and society and language will catch up with you eventually.

A-Z of sexual orientation

Asexual

Asexual is the term used to describe people who feel little or no sexual attraction to anyone. This is totally normal and may be more common than you think.

Bisexual

This is the term used to describe people who are sexually attracted to more than one gender. It is sometimes shortened to just 'bi'.

Biphobia

Biphobia is the word for the discrimination and prejudice that bisexual people face.

Closeted

This is a term used to describe when someone is not currently open with others about their sexual orientation or gender identity. How 'closeted' someone is may vary depending on the context. For example, some people may be closeted at work or school but not at home.

Coming out

This is the process of accepting your sexual orientation or gender identity, and becoming open about that with both yourself, and others.

Gay

This is used to describe people who are exclusively attracted to members of the same gender. Some gay women will prefer to refer to themselves as lesbians.

Heteronormative

Heteronormative is the term used to describe the belief that to be heterosexual and cisgender is the only natural way of living, and that anything else is outside of the norm, unusual or deviant.

Heterosexism

This is a form of prejudice or bias that believes that heterosexual relationships between cisgender people are somehow superior, more natural, or deserving of better treatment than gay or lesbian relationships, or relationships between transgender people.

Heterosexual

This the word used to describe someone who is exclusively attracted to members of the opposite gender.

Homophobia

Homophobia is a form of prejudice or discrimination faced by lesbian, gay and bisexual people.

Homosexual

This a word used to describe someone who is exclusively attracted to members of the same sex. Many gay and lesbian people will prefer to simply be referred to as gay or lesbian.

Lesbian

This is a word used to describe women who are exclusively attracted to other women. Some of these women will prefer to simply describe themselves as gay.

LGBTQIA+

LGBTQIA+ is a commonly used acronym for Lesbian, Gay, Bisexual, Transgender, Queer or Questioning, Intersex or Asexual. The + sign is to signify other categories of gender and sexual orientation that aren't accurately described by these terms.

MSM

An acronym for 'men who have sex with men'. People who fall under this category do not necessarily identify as gay or bisexual, but may be straight men who have had sexual experiences with men at different stages of their life.

Outing

This is when a person publicly declares someone else to be LGBTQIA+. It is often against the will of the LGBTQIA+ person.

Pansexual

This is used to describe someone who is attracted to people irrespective of gender identity and expression.

Pride

Pride is an international movement that encourages LGBTQIA+ people to celebrate their sexual orientation or gender identity, that challenges ongoing discrimination and oppression of LGBTQIA+ people, and that increases the public visibility of LGBTQIA+ people. In the UK, most Pride celebrations take place during the summer months.

Queer

Queer is an umbrella term used to describe people who do not fall into a traditional gender role or sexual orientation.

Essentially, it can be used to describe anyone who is not heterosexual and cisgender. However, it has historically been used as a slur against LGBTQIA+ people, and some will still be pretty offended by it. As such, it's only ok to use it about another person if that person self-identifies as queer.

Questioning

This is when someone is unsure of their sexual orientation or gender identity and are in the process of questioning it. Many people go through phases of questioning in their life, whether they're straight, gay, bi, lesbian, trans or cis, and this is absolutely fine.

Sexual orientation

Sexual orientation is a term used to describe what gender or genders someone is attracted to.

Straight

A term used to describe people who are exclusively attracted to members of the opposite gender. It can be used interchangeably with heterosexual.

One in five young people identify as gay, lesbian or bisexual

Britons more likely than ever to see themselves as somewhere between homosexual or heterosexual, with the number of 18-24s identifying as bisexual eight times higher than 2015.

By Victoria Waldersee

A new YouGov survey shows more people than ever identify as somewhere between the extremes of the sexuality spectrum, with those aged 18 to 24 now eight times more likely than they were in 2015 to identify as bisexual.

When we asked 18 to 24 year olds in to choose what best described their sexuality in 2015 just one in fifty (2%) said they were bisexual. Our latest data, from this month, shows that one in six (16%) now choose this option – an eight-fold increase.

Building on the idea of sexuality as a spectrum, YouGov asked Britons where they would place themselves on the Kinsey scale of 0 to 6, where 0 is completely heterosexual and 6 is completely homosexual.

The results show that when people are asked to identify themselves on a scale, rather than within a defined set of options (heterosexual, homosexual or bisexual), the number identifying as 'completely heterosexual' - 0 on the scale - falls from 86% to 72%.

On the whole, Britons are slightly more likely to place themselves somewhere in between the two extremes of 0 and 6 than they were in 2015. One in four (24%) place themselves between 1 and 5, compared to one in five (19%) four years ago. The change is grounded in people moving from choosing 0 – completely heterosexual – to choosing 1 or 2. Among 18 to 24s, of whom 16% chose 'bisexual' from a set of fixed options, a full 32% place themselves on '1' or '2'.

Among those who identified as 'heterosexual' in the first question of the survey, four in ten (41%) did not rule out that 'if the right person came along at the right time', it is conceivable that they could be attracted to a person of the same sex. A third (35%) could conceive of having a relationship with someone of the same sex – including one in ten (10%) of those who initially said there is 'no middle ground' in sexuality.

3 July 2019

18 to 24 year old half as likely to identify as gay or lesbian and eight times more likely to identify as bisexual as they were in 2015

Which of the following best describes your sexuality? % of 18-24 year olds

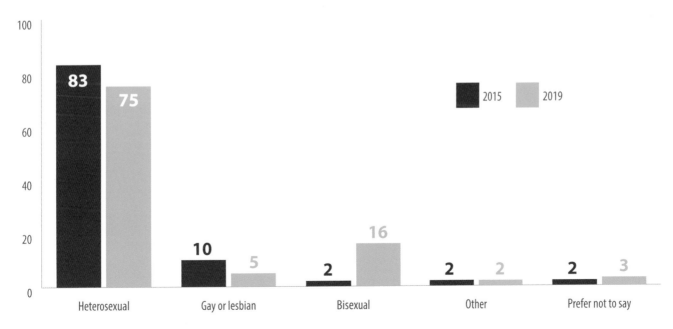

Source: YouGov, 13 -14 Aug 2015 / 23 -24 May 2019

One in five teens report change in sexual orientation during adolescence, study finds

Some teens who identified as heterosexual reported having some attraction to same sex or engaging in same-sex sexual behaviour.

By Chelsea Ritschel

Teenagers are likely to experience sexual fluidity during adolescence, with a new study finding one in five adolescents report change in sexual orientation or sexual attraction during that period of life.

According to researchers at North Carolina State University, the University of North Carolina at Chapel Hill and the University of Pittsburgh, adolescents are 'heterogeneous' when it comes to how they define and experience their sexual orientation.

To study how sexual orientation changes during adolescence, researchers analysed data from 744 high school students in the rural southern US based on three components: specific identity labels, romantic attractions, and other- and/or same-sex sexual behaviour.

The students, 54 per cent of which were girls and 46 per cent of which were boys, were asked to fill out surveys each year for three years.

The research found that at some point during the three-year period, 19 per cent of students reported at least one change in their self-labelled sexual identity.

According to researchers, this included changes such as students switching from identifying as heterosexual to bisexual.

Researchers found that female students were more likely to report a change in sexual identity, with 26 per cent reporting a change compared to just 11 per cent of male students.

The study also found differences between female and male students in regards to romantic attraction, with 21 per cent of the teenagers reporting changes in who they were attracted to over the course of the study. Female students made up the majority of these reports, in comparison to just 10 per cent of male students who reported changes in romantic attraction.

'This work highlights the fluidity that many adolescents experience in terms of how they label their sexuality and who they feel sexually attracted to,' said J Stewart, a PhD student at NC State and the lead author of the study. 'Some adolescents shifted between sexual minority identities and/ or attractions - gay or lesbian, bisexual, etc as well as varying degrees of same-sex attractions - across all three years.

'Others fluctuated between heterosexual and sexual minority groups. And when we looked at the extent to which sexual identity, attraction and sexual behaviour aligned, we saw some interesting trends.'

Even among students who identified as heterosexual, researchers found variability, with both male and female students reporting having some attraction to the same sex or engaging in same-sex sexual behaviour over the three-year period.

Of the findings, Stewart said: 'Adolescence is a time of identity exploration, and sexual orientation is one aspect of that. One takeaway here is that the process of sexual identity development is quite nuanced for a lot of teens. And based on research with young adults, we expect these patterns will continue for many people into their late 20s and even beyond.'

Stewart also said it is important to note that the findings were 'internally driven changes' and could not be 'imposed on an individual'.

'To be clear, we're talking about internally driven changes in sexual orientation,' he said. 'This research does not suggest these changes can be imposed on an individual and does not support the idea of conversion therapy. There's ample evidence that conversion therapy is harmful and does not influence anyone's sexual orientation.'

In the future, the researchers plan to expand the study, which was published in the Journal of Adolescence, across 'different sociopolitical environments'.

4 November 2019

10 tips on how to come out

Coming out is the terminology used to describe the process of sharing your sexuality/gender identity with the world. Many LGBTQ+ members struggle with sharing these personal details due to it being a sensitive topic.

Without knowing how friends/family will react to the news we're LGBTQ+, this uncertainty leaves us feeling anxious and frankly terrified to share the news… we're not straight. Speaking from my own personal experiences, my family/friends reacted positively and it was amazing to be accepted. But prior to this I still felt all of these emotions. So here are some tips on how to come out to your friends and family.

1. Be patient

What's so important is to be patient with yourself and others. Right now, you may be feeling so many emotions you may not truly understand what's going on. Sometimes we need time to process our emotions and come to terms with what's actually happening.

If you're not 100% or are confused, then don't panic. Be patient and reach out to fellow LGBTQ+ members to talk through what's going on. It may be that you just need that extra guidance before you come out to everyone and that's 100% okay.

2. Read coming out stories

Reading other coming out stories is an amazing way to explore different sexualities. Through others, we can learn so much and be prepared for scenarios that may occur. But most importantly, we see the other side of being open with our sexuality or gender identity.

We all face unique problems and through our stories we can help others prepare for certain situations.

3. Labels aren't for everyone

Labels come in the shape and form of Lesbian, Bisexual, Pansexual, Gay and so on. Trying to figure out our sexuality can be confusing, as sometimes labels overlap.

If you're struggling to figure out which sexuality suits you best, it's important to understand that you don't need a label to identify within the LGBTQ+ community and can still be as valid without labelling yourself. We sometimes feel pressured to come out with a label attached, but we simply can say we're not straight and still be as valid. Don't force yourself to be anything, just be you!

4. Do your own research

We live in an era of the internet and like ourselves, there are many blogs and social media pages where they give advice on coming out and other LGBTQ+ related situations. The more we educate ourselves on topics that affect us directly, we develop a self-awareness that prior, we didn't have.

We aren't taught LGBTQ+ topics and what we see in the mainstream media is sometimes an exaggeration of the truth. So my recommendation is to read real-life situations and understand that your sexuality/gender identity doesn't change your worth as a human being. Don't let anyone tell you any differently. No matter what, we are still equal to everyone else around us.

5. Talk to other LGBT+ people

The world is full of LGBTQ+ individuals who have all experienced coming out in different ways, so talk to them! We aren't scary and we have all been through the coming out process. So talk to us, ask questions and hear our stories. It will not only help you gain a further understanding of coming out, but you may make some friends along the way.

The LGBTQ+ community is here to love, support and help others. So, don't be frightened to reach out.

6. Expect the worst

Sometimes, we can't help the views of others. We have to accept that there will be people out there that will judge and discriminate against us, just because of our sexuality. Whether this be your parents or friends, it's not our fault they feel such strong hate towards the LGBTQ+ community.

When you come out, there will be individuals that can take it badly. You may get bullied, people will talk and things will get said to you. But, don't let this change who you are. In life, people will always talk and judge you so why not let them talk about you whilst you're happy being your true self.

When I accepted that I could never control others' views, I let go and started living my life for me. We only get one shot, there isn't enough time to worry about the ifs and buts. You have to do things for yourself and if you upset and lose people along the way, then that's their problem, not yours.

7. Confide in a close friend

Now, with this one you need to make sure that whoever you confide in will not tell anyone. You need to be able to trust this person with your life and they need to be able to keep this secret until you're ready. But, talking about your feelings out loud sometimes makes sense of what's going on in your head.

Getting it all out into the world, even if it's just to one person sometimes can change your whole attitude towards coming out. But if you don't have anyone to confide in then don't worry because we are here. If you ever need to talk about how you are feeling, we are active 24/7 and will always help and try give the best advice we can. So, just get in touch and we will get back to you asap.

8. Forget all you know about LGBTQ+ people

This one kind of links in with research, but you need to forget all of what you think you know about LGBTQ+ individuals. The media for so long has painted us in a certain light that stereotypes and myths plague the community. As ever, they aren't anything but fabricated lies and are complete bullsh*t.

Not all gay people act the same way, not all lesbians hate men and you know what, bisexuals aren't greedy! So, start afresh and do you. You don't have to be a certain way to identify within the LGBTQ+ community, you just need to be you.

9. You don't need to come out

The concept that when you've figured it all out & then you must come out, is so wrong because the reality is, you don't have to come out. We never see straight people go;

'Oh hey, by the way, I'm straight. I thought I should just let you know'

It's not a thing, so why should it be a thing for us? You don't have to ever come out if you don't want to, as coming out shouldn't really have to be a thing. But hey, that's for another post! All you need to do is be happy within yourself. If you're happy and content with who you are then you don't need to justify that to anyone, let alone the world.

10. Make sure you're happy

My final tip for coming out is… make sure at the end of all this that you're happy. Sometimes, we need to be selfish and think about our own happiness. If coming out will make you 100x happier, then do it for you. God yeah, there may be hurdles along the way. But in the end, you finally get to live your life how you intended.

This is your life, don't let others determine how you live. Be you, do you and be happy.

10 April 2018

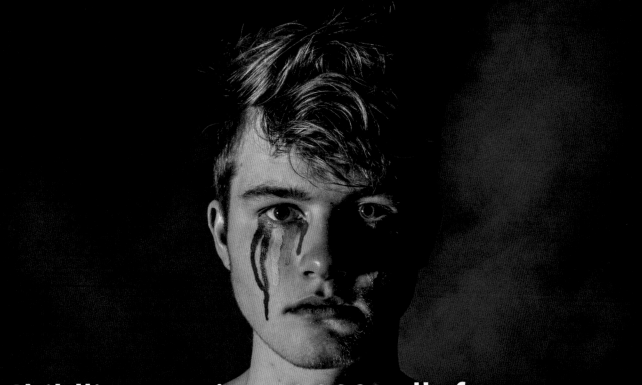

Childline receives 6,000 calls from young people struggling with sexuality and gender identity

Children as young as 11 were among those dealing with bullying and suicidal thoughts.

By Ewan Somerville

Children as young as 11 were among the 6,000 cries for help to Childline last year from young people struggling with their sexuality and gender identity.

Counsellors at Childline saw 16 cases each day related to sexuality and gender issues such as bullying and suicidal thoughts last year, with 409 of these among 11 year-olds or younger.

Children's charity NSPCC, which runs Childline, also saw a 40 per cent increase in young people struggling with 'coming out' to their parents between 2017-2018 and 2018-2019, and homophobic bullying was mentioned in 573 calls and emails to the service.

The Childline webpage advising those who identify as transgender saw an 80 per cent hike in page views in the last year alone.

'My parents don't understand me'

One boy told counsellors: 'I have been feeling depressed and suicidal for about three years. My parents don't understand me at all. I came out as Trans and they think it's just a phase and refuse to accept me. I am in pain.'

The new figures come during Pride month, with towns and cities nationwide seeing the LGBT+ community gather to celebrate difference and inclusivity - but the NSPCC stressed that help is available for those struggling.

'No-one should ever make you feel like you shouldn't exist because you feel differently to them,' Munroe Bergdorf, a Childline LGBTQ+ campaigner, said. 'Don't let anyone tell you that your emotions or feelings don't matter because if you hear it enough it will break you.'

Listen sensitively

Dame Esther Rantzen, founder of Childline, added: 'I know that some adults feel uncomfortable talking about these issues with young people, but if we create a taboo around them, that can make children feel guilty, rejected and in some cases has even led to depression and even suicide.

'We all need to listen sensitively and support young people and protect them from this profound unhappiness and loneliness.'

5 June 2019

> ## Childline
> Call free on 0800 111 or visit childline.org.uk for support, information and advice.

Sexual orientation, UK: 2018

Experimental statistics on sexual orientation in the UK in 2018 by region, sex, age, marital status, ethnicity and socio-economic classification.

Main points

- The proportion of the UK population aged 16 years and over identifying as heterosexual or straight decreased from 95.3% in 2014 to 94.6% in 2018.

- The proportion identifying as lesbian, gay or bisexual (LGB) increased from 1.6% in 2014 to 2.3% in 2018.

- In 2018, there were an estimated 1.2 million people aged 16 years and over identifying as LGB.

- Men (2.5%) were more likely to identify as LGB than women (2.0%) in 2018.

- Younger people (aged 16 to 24 years) were most likely to identify as LGB in 2018 (4.4%).

- Among English regions, people in London were most likely to identify as LGB (2.8%), with people in the North East the least likely (1.8%).

- More than two-thirds (68.7%) of people who identified as LGB were single (never married or in a civil partnership).

Statistician's comment

'People in their late teens and early twenties are more likely to identify as lesbian, gay or bisexual (LGB) than older age groups.

'Meanwhile, more than two-thirds of the LGB population are single (never married or entered into a civil partnership).

This reflects the younger age structure of this population, the changing attitudes of the general population to marriage and the fact that legal unions have only recently been available for same-sex couples.'

Sophie Sanders, Population Statistics Division, Office for National Statistics.

Sexual orientation in the UK

In 2018, an estimated 94.6% of the UK population aged 16 years and over (53.0 million people) identified as heterosexual or straight. This represents a continuation of the decrease seen since 2014, when 95.3% of the population identified themselves as heterosexual or straight (Table 1).

An estimated 2.3% of the population aged 16 years and over (1.2 million people) identified themselves as lesbian, gay or bisexual (LGB) in 2018; this is comprised of 1.4% identifying as gay or lesbian and 0.9% as bisexual (see Table 1). The proportion of the population identifying as LGB increased from 1.6% in 2014 to 2.3% in 2018 (Figure 1).

A higher proportion of men than women identify as LGB

In 2018, 2.5% of men identified themselves as LGB, compared with 2.0% of women. More than twice the proportion of men (1.9%) compared with women (0.9%) identified as gay or lesbian (Figure 2). Conversely, a higher proportion of women than men identified as bisexual, at 1.1% and 0.6% respectively. This represents a continuation of a trend that

Most people in the UK identify themselves as heterosexual or straight

Sexual orientation, as a percentage, UK, 2014 to 2018

Sexual orientation	2014	2015	2016	2017	2018
Heterosexual or straight	95.3	95.2	95.0	95.0	94.6
Gay or lesbian	1.1	1.2	1.2	1.3	1.4
Bisexual	0.5	0.7	0.8	0.8	0.9
Other	0.3	0.4	0.5	0.6	0.6
Do not know or refuse	2.8	2.6	2.5	2.3	2.5

Source: Office for National Statistics – Annual Population Survey. Table 1

A lower proportion of people identified as heterosexual and a higher proportion identified as lesbian, gay or bisexual in 2018

Change in self-identified sexual orientation, UK, 2014 to 2018

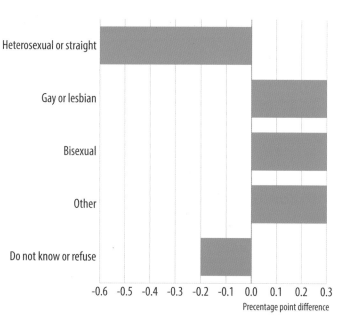

Source: Office for National Statistics – Annual Population Survey. Figure 1

Men were more likely to identify as gay or lesbian, while women were more likely to identify as bisexual

Lesbian, gay or bisexual population by sex, UK, 2018

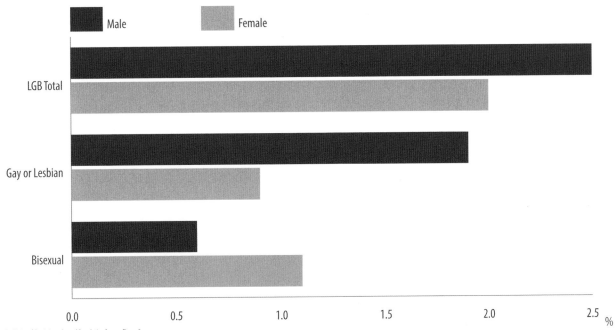

Source: Office for National Statistics – Annual Population Survey. Figure 2

has been observed back to 2014, where a higher proportion of men than women identify as gay or lesbian and a higher proportion of women than men identify as bisexual.

Sexual orientation by age

In 2018, people aged 16 to 24 years were more likely to identify as lesbian, gay or bisexual (LGB) than other age groups.

People in each successively older age group were less likely to identify as LGB than those in the preceding younger age group in 2018. Of the population aged 16 years and over, 20.9% of men and 23.4% of women are aged 65 years and over. However, only 6.7% of men and 7.4% of women who identified as LGB were aged 65 years and over. A possible reason for this pattern is that younger people could be more likely to explore their sexuality combined with more social

In 2018, a smaller proportion of people in Northern Ireland identified themselves as lesbian, gay or bisexual than in other UK countries

UK constituent countries by lesbian, gay or bisexual population, 2014 and 2018

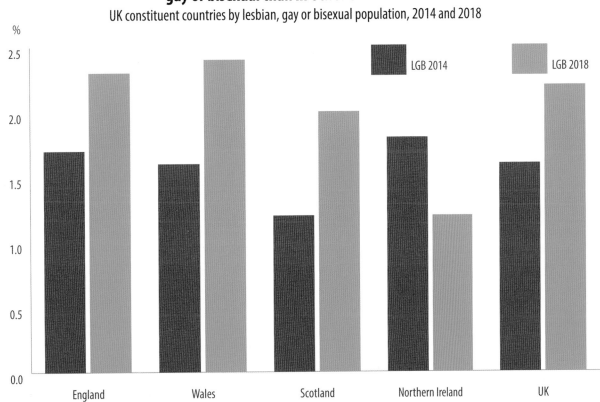

Source: Office for National Statistics – Annual Population Survey. Figure 4

A larger proportion of people in London identify as lesbian, gay or bisexual than in other English regions

English regions by lesbian, gay or bisexual population, 2014 and 2018

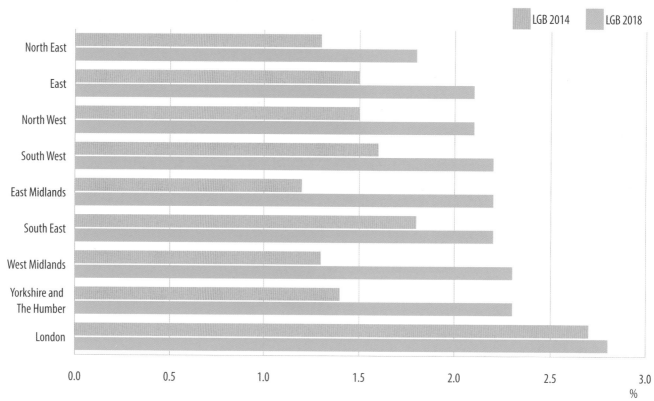

LGB 2014   LGB 2018

North East	
East	
North West	
South West	
East Midlands	
South East	
West Midlands	
Yorkshire and The Humber	
London	

0.0   0.5   1.0   1.5   2.0   2.5   3.0
%

Source: Office for National Statistics – Annual Population Survey. Figure 5

People identifying as lesbian, gay or bisexual are most likely to have a marital status of single (never married or civil partnered)

Lesbian, gay or bisexual population by legal marital status, UK, 2014 to 2018

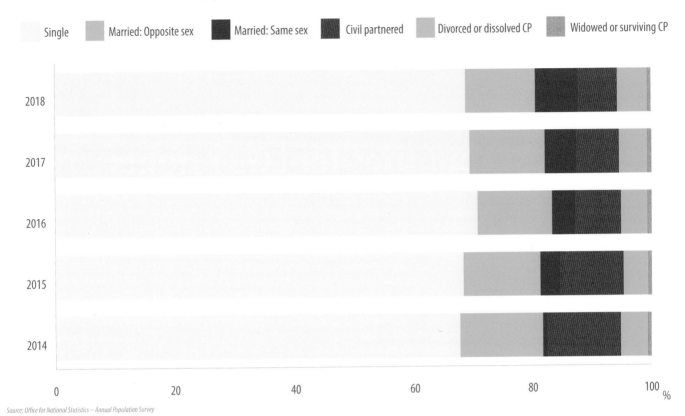

Source: Office for National Statistics – Annual Population Survey

acceptability of different sexual identities and the ability to express these today.

Sexual orientation by UK countries and English regions

In 2018, the percentage of people who identified as lesbian, gay or bisexual (LGB) was similar for England (2.3%), Wales (2.4%) and Scotland (2.0%).

For Northern Ireland, the percentage of people identifying themselves as LGB in 2018 was 1.2%. The UK average in 2018 was 2.3%, which has increased from 1.6% in 2014 (Figure 4).

The East Midlands and West Midlands were the regions that saw the largest change in the proportion of people identifying as LGB over the last four years, with both increasing from 2014 to 2018 (from 1.2% to 2.2% and 1.3% to 2.3% respectively) (Figure 5).

Sexual orientation by marital status

Among those identifying as lesbian, gay or bisexual (LGB) in 2018, more than two-thirds (68.7%) were single, meaning that they had never married or entered into a civil partnership. This is double the proportion of those who identified as heterosexual or straight and were single (34.2%). A possible reason for this difference is the younger age structure of the LGB population combined with the increase in the average age of marriage.

Furthermore, legal unions for same-sex couples have only become available recently; civil partnerships were introduced for same-sex couples in the UK in December 2005, and same-sex marriage has been available in England,

Wales and Scotland since 2014 and in Northern Ireland from 2020.

More couples are choosing to live together before or instead of marriage. Those with a legal marital status of single may live with a partner of the same or opposite sex. Same-sex cohabiting couples are the most common type of same-sex couple family, accounting for just over half of same-sex families in 2019.

From 2014 to 2018, the proportion of people identifying as LGB who were in same-sex marriages increased from 0.8% to 7.3%, while those in civil partnerships decreased from 12.3% to 6.5% (Figure 6). This suggests that since its introduction in 2014, an increasing number of people who identify as LGB are choosing to enter a same-sex marriage rather than a civil partnership or to convert their civil partnership to a same-sex marriage.

6 March 2020

The 10 best countries for LGBT rights

Lesbian, gay, bisexual and transgender (LGBT) rights can vary from country to country. Below is a list of countries who have made the greatest strides when it comes to protecting the rights of LGBT people.

By Joseph Kiprop

In recent decades, the recognition of LGBT rights has been of great concern in many parts of the world. Different countries or territories have their laws relating to lesbian, gay, bisexual, and transgender populations. Some of these laws recognize the LGBT community while others prescribe harsh punishments such as the death penalty.

Amnesty International is among the organizations which regard LGBT rights as human rights. Currently, about 22 nations recognize same-sex marriage, most of which lie in Western Europe and the Americas. This means that only about 10% of the world's population resides in a nation which recognizes same-sex marriage. Over 80 nations, on the other hand, have laws which facilitate the discrimination of LGBT individuals. In June 2015, Colombia represented 72 nations when it issued a joint statement to end discrimination and violence to LGBT people to the UN Human Rights Council. This is intended to pressure the world's nations to make strides in protecting LGBT citizens. In no particular order, here are ten countries who are paving the way.

10. Norway

In 1981, Norway adopted an anti-discrimination law which included sexual orientation. Same-sex marriage unions and adoption have been legally allowed since 2009 in addition to IVF therapy. Norway further approved a law which allows a person to change their legal sex. Norway is one of the most accepting countries in the world for LGBT travellers.

9. United Kingdom

The period between 1967 and 1982 was characterized by the decriminalisation of homosexuality across the UK. The 21st century in the UK has been marked by the adoption of protections for LGBT people. LGBT individuals can serve in the armed forces and the change of legal gender is allowed. England, Scotland, and Wales have since legalized same-sex marriage while Northern Ireland allows for a civil partnership. Protection from discrimination is provided for in laws of the country.

8. Finland

Although homosexuality only ceased to be regarded as an illness in 1981, Finland has made major strides in recognizing the rights of LGBT people since. The Finnish Parliament adopted a 2014 law which recognized same-sex marriage in addition to joint adoption by gay and lesbian couples. Furthermore, lesbian and gay people can openly work in Finland's military while transgender individuals can choose to switch to another legal gender. The country has also adopted numerous anti-discrimination laws for LGBT communities.

7. Denmark

Same-sex activity has been legal in Denmark since 1933, and the age of consent was adopted at 15 in 1977 regardless of gender or sexual orientation. Denmark made history in 1989 when it became the first nation to offer legal recognition to same-sex partnerships with the title 'registered partnerships'. A same-sex marriage law was officially adopted in 2012, and joint adoptions for those in same-sex marriages was approved in 2010. Copenhagen is frequently recognized as one of the world's most gay-friendly cities due to scenes such as the yearly Pride Parade. Denmark's autonomous territories of the Faroe Islands and Greenland have also legalized same-sex marriage.

6. Belgium

Same-sex activity in Belgium was legal from as far back as 1795 with an exception for the period between 1965 and 1985. Belgium was the 2nd country in the world to legally recognize same-sex marriage in 2003. In 2006, same-sex adoption became legal in the country while lesbian couples can access IVF. Belgium hosts some internationally renowned gay pride festivals such as La Démence. Cities like Brussels have a thriving LGBT scene which includes Pride Week.

5. Spain

The rights of LGBT individuals have received much attention in Spain from the late 20th century. Homosexuality became legal in 1979, and same-sex marriage gained legal recognition in 2005 along with adoption rights. The Pew Research Center estimates that 90% of Spain's population is of the view that gay and lesbian communities should be accepted. Barcelona has been identified as one of the friendliest metropolises in the world for LGBT individuals.

4. The Netherlands

When France invaded and occupied the territory of the Netherlands, it enacted the Napoleonic code which legalized same-sex relationships and erased discriminatory laws. The Netherlands did not institute any laws criminalising same-sex relations after independence. As LGBT rights gained societal recognition in the late 20th century, homosexuality was removed from the official list of illnesses in 1973. In 2001, the Netherlands became one of the first countries in the world to legalize same-sex marriage. Amsterdam has a reputation as a very LGBT-friendly city.

3. Malta

Malta has been lauded for its LGBT rights and awareness. It was named by the International Lesbian, Gay, Bisexual, Trans and Intersex Association as Europe's most LGBT-friendly country. Rights for LGBT is part of the country's constitution. Since 2004, Malta has banned all discrimination on the grounds of gender identity and expression and sexual orientation. LGBT citizens can openly serve in Malta's military and a law enacted in 2014 gives these people the right to be in civil unions. Most notably, Malta has banned conversion therapy. However, it has been reported that access to reproduction assistance and surrogacy are still banned for same-sex couples in Malta. As of 2017, same-sex marriage in Malta is legal.

2. Portugal

LGBT rights have risen to prominence in Portuguese society, and have made major improvements in recent years. Legally speaking, homosexuality could no longer be prosecuted by law as of 1983, and same-sex marriage was legalized in 2010. Portugal has numerous anti-discrimination laws which are intended to ensure that LGBT citizens enjoy equal rights to everyone else.

1. Canada

The last person to be imprisoned on accounts of homosexuality in Canada was named Everett George Klippert. Klippert's case resulted in the decriminalisation of homosexuality in Canada in 1969. Canada adopted the Civil Marriage Act in 2005 which made it legal for same-sex couples to get married. Transgender individuals can change their legal gender in all territories and provinces under varying regulations. As of 2017, Canada made strides by allowing its citizens to choose a third sex, called 'X', on their Canadian passport. Polls have revealed that LGBT rights are accepted by the vast majority of Canadian society. Canadian cities such as Ottawa, Toronto, Vancouver, and Montreal even have 'gay villages' and are often included as gay-friendly cities.

31 May 2019

Legalising homosexuality: Germany did it 25 years ago - what about other European countries?

By Anne Fleischmann

This week Germany celebrated legalising homosexuality twenty-five years ago.

Until June 11, 1994, it was still considered a crime in Germany even though since 1969 homosexuals were no longer prosecuted for 'fornication'.

Eighteen years ago, it became legal for same-sex couples in Germany to register their partnership and since 2015, people in a partnership can adopt their partner's child. Two years later, same-sex marriage became legal (Eheöffnungsgesetz).

Compared to many other European countries, Germany was quite late to legalise homosexuality.

Euronews takes a look at homosexuality laws across Europe.

Austria

Until 1971 homosexuality was punishable in Austria and until 2002 there were still minimum age limits for homosexual relationships in the Austrian penal code (different from heterosexual relationships). The code allowed heterosexual partnerships to start at the age of 14, however, homosexual relationships were only considered legal from the age of 18 onwards.

This section in the code only concerned male same-sex couples.

The Constitutional Court pleaded for the paragraph to be repealed and set a deadline for Parliament until 2003. This eventually led to the end of discrimination against homosexuals.

The country has allowed registered partnerships (Eingetragene Partnerschaft) since January 1, 2010, and same-sex marriage for all couples became legal on January 1, 2019.

Switzerland

Homosexuality has been legal in Switzerland since 1942. The minimum legal age of 20 for homosexual relationships (as opposed to 16 for heterosexual relationships) was lifted at the end of 1990.

Same-sex marriage is currently illegal in Switzerland. Since 2007, same-sex couples can opt to register their partnership and enjoy many of the same rights and obligations as married couples.

However, they do not allow the adoption of children or allow couples to have children using artificial insemination.

People in a registered partnership can, however, adopt their partner's child from a previous relationship.

Italy

Thanks to the criminal code by Justice Minister Giuseppe Zanardelli — the so-called Zanardelli Code — homosexuality was decriminalised in 1889. Since then, homosexuality has been considered a 'sin against religion and privacy' as long as it did not involve violence or public scandals. But homosexuality itself is not prosecuted.

But what might seem like a liberal code at first glance was, in fact, a strategy to keep homosexuality away from public life. Although there was no criminal repression against homosexuality, same-sex couples were not persecuted as long as they kept their private life behind closed doors.

The 1930's Rocco code reinforced this approach. The legal text read: 'It will not be punished because the vicious vice of homosexuality in Italy is not so widespread that it requires legal intervention.'

This approach of turning a blind eye is still widespread today. In several African countries, such as Uganda, heads of state deny that there are homosexuals in their country even though they still persecute them.

France

The French law of August 4, 1982, put an end to the prohibition of homosexual relations between an adult and a minor over fifteen years of age — a measure taken by the Vichy regime in 1942.

And since 1981, France no longer classifies homosexuality as a mental illness (while WHO did not remove it from its list until May 1993).

However, homosexuality was never officially banned in France. Until 1791, sodomy was banned, but not explicitly homosexual relationships. However, the prohibition of sodomy was used to sentence homosexuals to death and burn them at the stake.

In 2013, same-sex marriage and adoption became legal in France.

Spain

In Spain, homosexuality was no longer considered a criminal offence from 1978 onwards.

Same-sex marriage was legalised in 2005 in Spain — making it one of the first European countries, along with Belgium (2003) and the Netherlands (2001), to legalise same-sex marriage.

UK

The pioneers in LGBT rights in the UK have been England and Wales who legalised homosexuality in 1967 (Sexual Offences Act 1967).

Homosexual acts in Scotland were decriminalised by the Criminal Justice Scotland Act 1980, which took effect on February 1 1981.

In Northern Ireland, homosexuality was legalised in 1982 (Homosexual Offences (Northern Ireland) Order 1982).

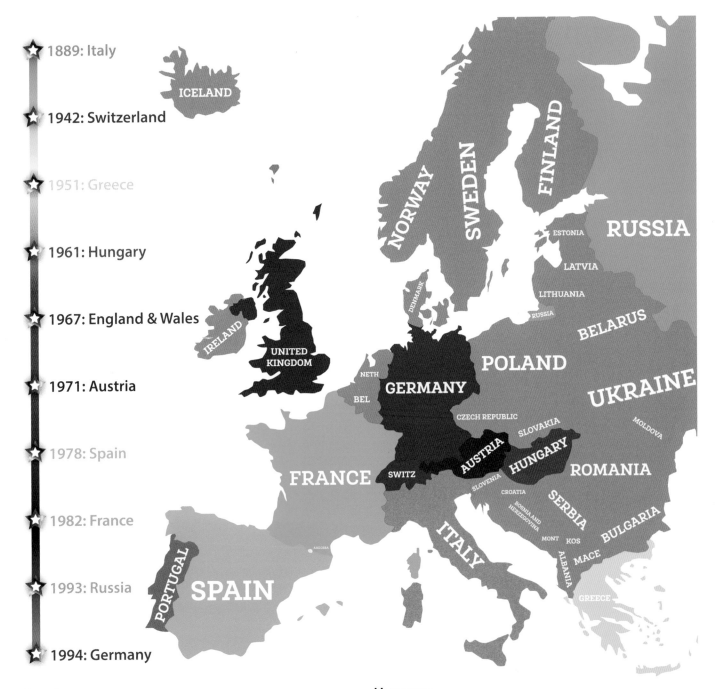

Timeline:

- 1889: Italy
- 1942: Switzerland
- 1951: Greece
- 1961: Hungary
- 1967: England & Wales
- 1971: Austria
- 1978: Spain
- 1982: France
- 1993: Russia
- 1994: Germany

Russia

Homosexuality was decriminalised after the Russian revolution in the early 1920s.

However, under Stalin, homosexuality became punishable again in 1937.

It was not until 1993 that the law was repealed and homosexuality decriminalised.

In 2013, the State Duma passed a law banning any form of 'gay propaganda'. The official title of the law is 'The Russian federal law for the Purpose of Protecting Children from Information Advocating for a Denial of Traditional Family Values'.

Greece

In Greece homosexuality has not been a criminal offence since 1951. A specific article within the law specifically punishing sex between men in cases of prostitution or if one of the partners was a minor was abolished in 2015.

That same year, same-sex unions became legal.

Hungary

In Hungary, homosexuality was decriminalised in 1961. The Austrian Emperor Josef II, who was also the ruler of Hungary, lifted the death penalty for homosexuals in 1787.

However, same-sex couples in Hungary cannot get married. In 2012, marriage was defined in the Hungarian constitution as between a man and a woman.

Amendments have so far been unsuccessful.

14 June 2019

8 reasons why 2020 is a huge year for LGBTI rights

2019 was eventful – at times hugely challenging.

There were incredible steps forward for LGBTI rights around the world. Austria, Taiwan, Ecuador and Northern Ireland all legalised same-sex marriage.

2020 will likely be equally busy. Here are eight legal cases coming up that we'll be keeping a close eye on.

United States

The US Supreme Court is set to decide whether LGBTI people are protected from discrimination at work by the 1964 Civil Rights Act.

Access to bathrooms for transgender students will be back in the news.

HIV-positive military personnel, who were dismissed or banned from service, will have their case against the Pentagon heard.

Botswana

The government is appealing last year's High Court ruling that decriminalised gay sex. A decision is expected later this year.

Previously, same-sex relationships could be punished with up to seven years in prison.

Singapore

At least three men have launched legal bids to decriminalise colonial-era bans on gay sex on the grounds either that it's unconstitutional or violates human dignity.

Roy Tan, a retired doctor, is 'eager to see this archaic law, which has no place in modern society', struck down.

He said: 'By institutionalising discrimination, it alienates them [LGBTI people] from having a sense of belonging and purposeful place in our society, and prevents them from taking pride in Singapore's achievements.'

Jamaica

Another country striving to overturn old homophobic laws is Jamaica.

The Inter-American Commission on Human Rights (IACHR) have lodged a petition that – while not being legally binding – could send shock waves throughout the region.

Campaigners are challenging similar colonial 'buggery laws' in Antigua and Barbuda, St Kitts and Nevis, Saint Lucia, Grenada, Saint Vincent and the Grenadines and Dominica too.

Barbados

A law punishing sex between men with life imprisonment was challenged in 2018 by the IACHR.

They're still waiting to hear back from the government, but if the commission recommends reform and the government refuses, the matter could be escalated to the Inter-American Court of Human Rights.

Hong Kong

Homosexuality has been decriminalised in Hong Kong since 1991. Now two cases aim to bring same-sex marriage to the city, despite an October judgement stating that there was no obligation to allow LGBTI unions.

Kenya

In May 2019 the High Court ruled to keep the ban on gay sex, which is punishable by 14 years in jail.

The National Gay & Lesbian Human Rights Commission disagree and are appealing the judgement.

Europe

Last year we handed in our 300k signature petition to Russian authorities calling on President Putin to end the persecution of LGBTI people in Chechnya.

This year the European Court of Human Rights is looking at the case of a gay man who said he was persecuted in Chechnya, as well as holding an inquiry into a series of arrests in 2017 of LGBTI people in Azerbaijan.

15 January 2020

First same-sex marriage takes place in Northern Ireland

Belfast couple Robyn Peoples and Sharni Edwards make history after law change.

A Belfast couple have tied the knot in the first same-sex marriage to take place in Northern Ireland.

Robyn Peoples, 26, and Sharni Edwards, 27, made history at a ceremony in a hotel in Carrickfergus, County Antrim, on Tuesday afternoon. Their marriage came after a law change in the region.

The day marks their sixth anniversary as a couple and they had booked a civil partnership ceremony at the Loughshore hotel months before the legislation was passed last summer.

When it became clear the first marriages could take place in Northern Ireland this week, they changed their ceremony to a wedding.

After a long and high-profile campaign for change, same-sex marriage was legalised at Westminster by MPs who stepped in and acted on the issue during the power-sharing impasse at Stormont.

Edwards said 'it means the absolute world' to be married, before thanking the activists who have campaigned for same-sex marriage in Northern Ireland.

'If it wasn't for them guys we wouldn't be sat here right now. We just want to say thank you to everyone... everyone who has marched and signed petitions, everyone who has helped us get to this stage, we just want to say thank you.

'We didn't expect to be the first couple, it's coincidental. Today is our six-year anniversary so we wanted to go ahead with a civil partnership but when the bill was passed it was perfect timing and it was a complete coincidence, a happy coincidence. We couldn't be more grateful.'

Peoples said: 'For Northern Ireland, we need to be the face of the people to show everyone it's OK. We fought so long and hard for this opportunity to be seen as equal and now we are here and it's just amazing.'

Edwards, a waitress from Brighton who did not know the law was different in Northern Ireland until she moved from England to Belfast, said: 'We feel humbled that our wedding is a landmark moment for equal rights in Northern Ireland. We didn't set out to make history – we just fell in love.

'We are so grateful to the thousands of people who marched for our freedoms, to the Love Equality campaign who led the way, and the politicians who voted to change the law. Without you, our wedding wouldn't have been possible. We will be forever thankful.'

Just Married

While the wedding took place in County Antrim, at Westminster campaigners were preparing for a celebratory reception to thank those MPs who acted on the issue.

Sara Canning, the partner of murdered author Lyra McKee, who was shot dead by dissident republicans in Londonderry last April, is attending the event organised by Amnesty International and the Love Equality campaign.

'What a wonderful moment in our history,' she said. 'This really means so much and has brought me some much-needed light in what has been a dark year.

'I know Lyra would have been so overjoyed to see this day … Of course, this historic moment is a little bittersweet. It had been our dream too. Lyra and I should have been an engaged couple now, planning our own wedding day.

'But I am so happy for Robyn and Sharni … and for all the other couples who will follow.'

11 February 2020

Homophobic and transphobic hate crimes surge in England and Wales

Offences double since 2014 against gay and lesbian people and treble against trans people, Guardian analysis reveals.

By Sarah Marsh, Aamna Mohdin and Niamh McIntyre

Homophobic and transphobic hate crimes, including stalking, harassment and violent assault, have more than doubled in England and Wales over five years, a Guardian analysis has shown.

The rate of LGBT hate crime per capita rose by 144% between 2013-14 and 2017-18. In the most recent year of data, police recorded 11,600 crimes, more than doubling from 4,600 during this period.

Transphobic attacks have soared in recent years, trebling from 550 reports to 1,650 over the period examined. Almost half (46%) of these crimes in 2017-2018 were violent offences, ranging from common assault to grievous bodily harm.

The findings come after two women were attacked on a bus in London for refusing to kiss in front of a group of men. The incident sparked widespread condemnation.

'When this happened, we were really angry,' says Melania Geymonat, 28. 'And we decided to tell the story, because this situation needs to change, and maybe this helps a little. For me, it was a moral obligation. Like, this needs to stop. This was a terrible episode, and maybe [if] we say something, we can contribute to something bigger.'

In 2017-18, 40% of anti-gay and lesbian hate crime in England and Wales were violence against a person. And more recent data released to the Guardian by Essex, Kent and Merseyside police forces appears to show the trend continuing.

In Kent, police reported a 42% annual rise in the number of LGBT hate crimes in 2018-2019, while Essex and Merseyside reported increases of 35% and 25% respectively.

Campaigners said the rise could partly be down to better reporting but added that hatred was growing on British streets because of the rise of right-wing populism.

Taz Edwards-White, an alliance manager at Metro, an equalities and diversity organisation, said the hate crime figures were likely to be 'the tip of the iceberg'.

She added: 'There is a tension, and even within our own LGBT community there is a tension. I believe it's a direct result of people feeling unsafe due to rise of the rightwing political movement.

'What we see in our services is lots of people experience day-to-day verbal attacks or violence and aggressive language and homophobic attitudes ... We do believe the political climate has had an impact: people feel unsafe. What is

Reports of anti-gay and lesbian hate crimes have more than doubled in five years

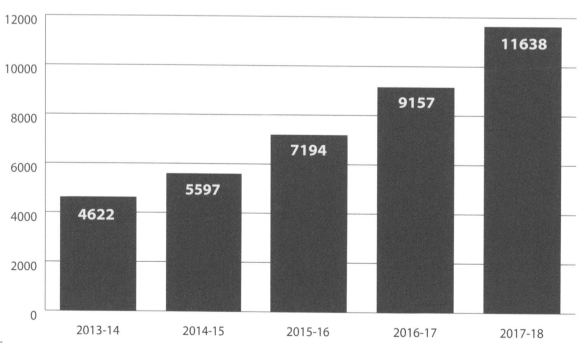

Year	Reports
2013-14	4622
2014-15	5597
2015-16	7194
2016-17	9157
2017-18	11638

Source: Home Office

Hate crimes against transgender people have trebled since 2013-14

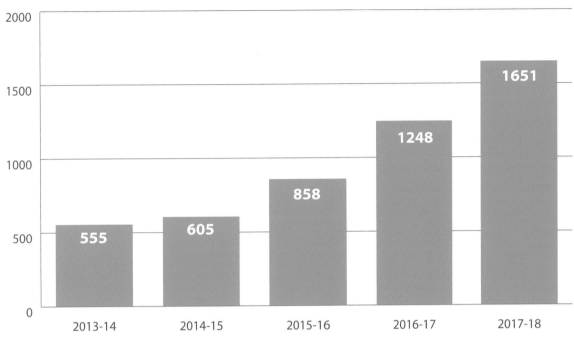

Source: Home Office

happening in central government and all the scapegoating has an effect. We saw a spike [in racist attacks] after Brexit and there has been a steady increase since then.'

Jessica White, who leads hate crime reporting work at the LGBT Foundation, an organisation based in Manchester, said the rise could be linked to an increased awareness of hate crime and its reporting.

She said: 'More and more, we are having people come to us who have been experiencing hate for a long period of time – prolonged abuse, often in their communities – who are finally coming forward to report. These will often be people who have been experiencing hate for years, see a poster on the tram, on the bus or on the train and realise that it's not okay and there is support there for them.'

The biggest increase in hate crime was in West Yorkshire, with the rate increasing by 376% between 2013-2014 and 2017-2018. On a regional level, the rate of anti-gay and lesbian crime trebled in Yorkshire and the Humber and the South East.

The analysis excluded all police force areas where fewer than 100 sexual orientation hate crimes were recorded in 2013-2014, and worked out the increase in the rate of crimes per 10,000 people up to 2017-2018.

Nick Antjoule, the head of hate crime services at Galop, an LGBT anti-violence charity, said the Guardian analysis came as no surprise. He said: 'We've seen a big spike in the scale and seriousness of hate crimes.'

Antjoule called for more specialist services to support LGBT people who experienced hate crimes, pointing to previous research by the Metropolitan police that showed victims of homophobic hate crime were more likely to experience more serious violence than victims of other forms of hate crimes.

He added: 'In the last several years, there's been a really huge spike in transphobic hostility that people are facing from their neighbours, public transport and online … It's something we need to see changed so people can live their lives openly.'

Laura Russell, the director of campaigns policy and research at Stonewall, said the rise in hate crimes showed there was a long way to go before the LGBT community was accepted in British society. 'We are still not living in a society where every LGBT person is able to achieve their potential and not have to live in fear of physical or verbal violence for being who they are,' she said.

In Hampshire, where two actors were recently attacked in a high-profile homophobic incident, the rate of homophobic hate crime increased 189% in the last five years – significantly higher than the England and Wales rate.

Hampshire police recorded 424 crimes in 2017-2018, up from 143 five years previously.

Race has consistently accounted for the majority of hate crimes reported to police in England and Wales. In the most recent year of data, race was a factor in 76% of crimes, compared to just over 12% in the sexual orientation category.

14 June 2019

We are gay Muslims and our voices need to be heard

The importance of sharing the voices of LGBT Muslims is huge - you can't speak about Muslim people as a homogeneous group.

By Ruchira Sharma

Ezra Stripe, 27, is a transgender lesbian Muslim living in England. They are one of six volunteers at Hidayah, a UK organisation for LGBTQI+ Muslims which campaigns against stigma, taboo and discrimination within the community.

Over the last month, Parkfield Community School in Birmingham made headlines after a new programme included lessons on LGBT rights and homophobia, sparking protests from Muslim parents who threatened to pull their children from school. Stripe spoke to Ruchira Sharma about the importance of giving LGBT Muslim voices a platform.

This past month, Parkfield Community School in Birmingham found itself at the centre of a national debate over Islam and homosexuality.

The school halted a new programme which included LGBT lessons until after Easter after some Muslim parents began withdrawing their children from class on what they argued was a religious and ethical basis.

The No Outsiders project was started by the assistant headteacher Andrew Moffat in an attempt to challenge homophobia in primary schools. Sadly he and the initiative came under fire from some Muslim parents who claimed homosexual relationships were strictly forbidden in Islam. They feared the lessons were immoral.

Being gay and Muslim is second nature

For me and many like me, it's been really disheartening to see the airtime the Parkfield protests are getting. It's frustrating knowing those kids are getting such a completely wrong message. What should have been a chance to promote tolerance and acceptance suddenly became a battleground among parents and teachers with LGBT identity at the centre.

In reality, there are people in the middle of the divide and people for whom it is second nature to be both gay and Muslim.

At the start of the protests, Hidayah reached out to news agencies but we weren't asked for our input. We've since done a few interviews, but we still haven't had enough of a platform.

The importance of sharing the voices of LGBT Muslims is huge. One of the things we see quite widely in our communities is feelings of shame, feelings of confusion and isolation. LGBT Muslims are fed messages that what they're doing is wrong.

Teaching children about multiple opinions

Sometimes we are even erased and the word 'gay' is never even mentioned at home - it is noted by omission that we don't exist, that gay Muslims aren't a thing as you cannot be both.

Secondary schools from around the country often invite us in to speak to them, but it can be really difficult to manage what parents have taught their children and the message of tolerance we promote. Many are astonished to see us as they've been told you cannot be gay and Muslim.

Once, I had a boy with autism ask me to write a note to his mum telling her that being gay isn't sinful and she was mistaken. That's not something I can do.

What we can and will do is tell students that we're here and there are different opinions, that their parents might have one view but that's not the only one. We try to not say 'your parents are wrong about this' or 'the lessons you've learnt are wrong' but that they are opinions. These are subject to each individual person's biases and they can form their own. There are many ways of being Muslim, some of which allow for people to be LGBT - it doesn't have to be mutually exclusive.

Homophobia doesn't have to be part of Islam

A lot of the ideas about religion and Islam specifically are based on very conservative, old-fashioned ideas.

The irony is that this culture of anti-homosexuality hasn't always been the case for Muslims. There's also a rich history of gender variance and homosexuality within Islam but it's all been wiped out by colonialism and sidelined in history.

Ultimately, Islam has a homophobia problem - it's no secret. But the reality is it's a cultural problem, not a religious one. In hiding behind the religion, protesters are being disingenuous. In order for any conversation to move forward, we need to accept Islam is divided in many ways by opinion - you can't speak about Muslim people as a homogeneous group. The parents are acting on an opinion of what they think the religion is, not necessarily what it is.

An issue of Muslim pride

On the surface, some parents are protesting the fact they weren't consulted properly. I think for many, nothing would have been good enough. It's a misplaced sense of Muslim pride; it's almost become as if they're protesting for the right to be Muslim and for their community instead of the original reason.

It feels like they're all standing together to say, 'no this is our community' and it's about much more than Parkfield. Both sides have to be willing to give some ground in order for this conversation to work.

My religion, sexuality and gender identity are crucial to me, primarily because they do exist in harmony. I don't claim my interpretation of Islam is the correct one but it makes it possible for those three things to live in harmony and to coexist in a way that benefits them all. I would hope every other LGBT Muslim feels the same.

6 September 2019

www.inews.co.uk

Faith and LGBT inclusion

By Ruth Hunt, Chief Executive

Faith is an important part of many LGBT people's lives, including my own. But this idea that keeps being perpetuated that LGBT people cannot possibly belong within faith communities has been deeply damaging. Stonewall research found that a third of lesbian, gay and bi people of faith (32 per cent) aren't open with anyone in their faith community about their sexual orientation. While one in four trans people of faith (25 per cent) aren't open about who they are in their faith community.

Faith has this almost unparalleled ability to bring people from all walks of life together in the name of love. LGBT people of faith need to be respected and included in their faith communities, just as they need respect and acceptance in wider society.

Amid the protests taking place at Parkfield Community School in Birmingham, it's been incredibly powerful to see and hear LGBT Muslims and allies standing up to affirm their support for LGBT-inclusive education. As Masuma Rahim rightly put it: 'Schools do, however, have a responsibility to teach children how to live in a society that is made up of people who will have some similarities to them, as well as those who will have differences.'

> **'Some children have no idea that it's even possible to be both gay and Muslim'**

It's vital children from all faith backgrounds learn about and celebrate diversity at all ages. As Ezra Stripe, diversity and inclusion officer at Hidayah, said: 'Some children have no idea that it's even possible to be both gay and Muslim. They've never been given space to explore these topics, and no one has ever sat them down and told them "actually, being LGBT is okay".'

We also cannot lose sight of the fact that many faith leaders and groups are already doing this crucial work in schools and local communities to promote love and messages of inclusivity. Like Benali Hamdache wrote: 'I know LGBT Muslims warmly accepted by their families… LGBT kids at Parkfield deserve to be supported in who they are'. Groups like Imaan LGBTQI have also been vocal in their support for inclusion of LGBT Muslims.

> **'LGBT kids at Parkfield deserve to be supported in who they are'**

The situation in Birmingham is also being used by some groups to further inflame Islamophobic attitudes. We must be vigilant to this and push against those who seek to sow division.

Stonewall's work has always focused on building bridges between communities to create a more accepting world for all LGBT people. We work closely with many faith schools and faith communities around the country to help them deliver LGBT-inclusive education to children and young people.

We're proud of the work we do with faith communities and schools to fight for LGBT equality. We know there are different opinions within faith communities, particularly when it comes to sexual orientation and gender identity. However, our support for LGBT people of faith's rights is unequivocal and - like our work on trans inclusion - cannot be debated.

Stonewall will continue to stand with LGBT people of all faiths. Building an equal society is about ensuring everyone in that society can access equality. We cannot leave people behind, we must ensure we are standing for and by everyone in our community.

8 March 2019

Young trans people in Britain

By Joël Reland

Claim

45% of young trans people in this country, have attempted suicide.

'45% of young trans people in this country, modern Britain, have attempted suicide. Not thought about, attempted'. – Paris Lees, 22 March 2018

We can't say for sure whether 45% of young trans people in Britain have tried to take their own life. It's not clear that the survey this claim is based on is representative of all young trans people in Britain.

45% of young trans people who took part in a survey commissioned by the LGBT charity Stonewall said they had at some point attempted to take their own life. 92% said they have thought about doing so. There were 594 young trans respondents overall.

Stonewall surveyed 3,713 young people aged 11 to 19 across Britain, from November 2016 to February 2017. The survey was for young people who are lesbian, gay, bi or trans, or who think they might be. 16% of those surveyed reported themselves to be trans.

That's a reasonable sample size, but we can't say if the people responding are representative of young LGBT people in Britain as a whole.

That's because we don't have information on the demographic profile of the young LGBT community overall, and so the researchers weren't able to adjust the findings to try and make them reflective of the general LGBT population.

Stonewall told us the survey was conducted via open recruitment and was self-selecting—in other words people chose whether to participate or not. This can be a problem in surveys because we don't know if certain types of person are more likely to respond in the first place—skewing the results.

The survey did take steps to mitigate this as well. Stonewall told us the survey was sent out with the aim of sounding as neutral in tone as possible, with the line 'what's life in Britain like for you?', and respondents were told there would be questions on school, and social life, role models and aspirations for the future.

The survey also provides some detail on the makeup of the respondents, in terms of the type of schools they attend, their ethnicity, their free school meal status, and whether or not they have a disability. However, this doesn't tell us if they are representative of the young LGBT community.

Conclusion

We can't say how representative this is of the young trans community in Britain as a whole—the overall sample was not adjusted to try and be representative. It's based on a survey of LGBT people aged 11 to 19, with 594 young trans respondents.

23 March 2018

LGBT+ youth four times more likely to self-harm than heterosexual peers

Scientists believe that more role models are needed for sexual-minority youth.

By Sabrina Barr

Children as young as ten who don't identify as heterosexual have a greater probability of experiencing symptoms of depression, new research has uncovered.

Approximately one in 25 people aged between 16 and 24 in the UK identify as lesbian, gay or bisexual, according to the Office for National Statistics.

While it's previously been discovered that young members of the LGBT+ community are more likely than those who identify as heterosexual to self-harm or experience depression, there hasn't been a substantial amount of research pinpointing when these mental health issues appear or how they progress over the years.

In a new study published in *The Lancet Child and Adolescent Health* journal, researchers compared the symptoms of depression exhibited by adolescents who are in a sexual minority with those who are heterosexual.

The authors have expressed their opinion that more mentors and role models are needed for sexual-minority youth, especially if they may be experiencing discrimination or stigma.

Individuals in sexual minorities include those who identify as gay, lesbian, bisexual, not exclusively heterosexual or haven't defined their sexual orientation.

The researchers followed almost 5,000 adolescents over the course of 11 years, noting depressive symptoms at seven points between the ages of 10 and 21 with a questionnaire.

The scientists from University College London also had the participants fill out a self-harm questionnaire at the age of 16 and then again at the age of 21.

All of the participants were born between 1 April 1991 and 31 December 1992 and reported their sexual orientation at the age of 16.

The team found that symptoms of depression were far more prevalent at the age of 10 among those in sexual minorities.

Furthermore, these symptoms were then likely to become worse during their teenage years and continue as they became young adults.

The authors noted that symptoms of depression among the sexual-minority youth began to lessen from the age of 18, which they state could be due to the teens becoming more independent or making new friends.

When the scientists had the participants fill out the self-harm questionnaire, they discovered that the young people in sexual minorities were four times more likely to have reported self-harming in the previous year than those who identify as heterosexual, and more than four times as likely to have reported self-harming with the aim of taking their own lives at the age of 21.

In October 2017, a study conducted by the University of Manchester revealed that incidents of self-harm among teenage girls had risen by 68 per cent in three years.

Moreover, research published by the Children's Society in August 2018 estimated that nearly 110,000 children aged 14 across the UK may have self-harmed in the past year, with the statistic consisting of 76,000 girls and 33,000 boys.

While the study conducted by University College London was observational, the authors have stated their belief that the stigma and discrimination that many members of the LGBT+ community face may be having a negative impact on the mental health of sexual-minority youth.

'The lack of sexual-minority role models and unquestioning acceptance of rigid concepts of gendered behaviour should be challenged in schools and society at large,' says Dr Glyn Lewis, professor of epidemiological psychiatry at UCL.

'We also need to ensure that doctors and those working in mental health are aware of this inequality and recognise the needs of sexual minorities.'

Dr Rohan Borschmann, psychologist at the Murdoch Children's Research Institute in Melbourne, Australia, believes that healthcare professionals and those who are in charge of making health policies should take heed of the study's findings in order to take better care of the mental health of young people.

'Irrespective of the exact nature of the relationship between sexual orientation and mental health, sexual-minority young people with mental health problems might experience double stigmatisation and it is well-established that discrimination and stigma are associated with decreased health outcomes,' he says.

'Reducing stigma and discrimination could, therefore, provide a pathway to primary prevention of mental disorders, by reducing the burden of disease, improving public health, and reducing health inequities.'

He also explains that self-harm and suicide prevention programmes should be geared specifically towards those who are most at risk or have personal experience with those particular issues.

12 December 2018

'Worryingly high' levels of body image anxiety in the LGBT+ community revealed in new Mental Health Foundation poll

Worryingly high numbers of people among the LGBT+ community have experienced body-image anxiety, a new online survey from the Mental Health Foundation has revealed. Of all the groups surveyed in the UK, the lesbian, gay and bisexual community appears to be the one most likely to be affected in this way.

One third (33 per cent) of the LGBT+ community said they had experienced suicidal thoughts and feelings in relation to their body image.

Nearly four in ten (39 per cent) of people who identified as bisexual and almost a quarter (23 per cent) of people who identified as gay or lesbian have experienced suicidal thoughts and feelings because of concerns about their body image. This compares to around one in ten (11 per cent) of heterosexuals.

Almost half (45 per cent) of people who identified as bisexual and nearly three in ten (29 per cent) people who identified as gay or lesbian have felt 'disgusted' because of their body image over the last year.

The survey was commissioned to mark Mental Health Awareness Week from 13-19 May, which this year has the theme of body image.

Other survey findings show that 29 per cent of bisexuals surveyed have deliberately hurt themselves because of their body image, as have 15 per cent of gay men and lesbians.

59 per cent of bisexuals and 46 per cent of gay men or lesbians felt 'anxious' because of their body image.

66 per cent of bisexuals have felt 'depressed' because of their body image, as have 45 per cent of gay men and lesbians.

Research has found that gay men are more likely than their heterosexual counterparts to experience a desire to be thin, and this can sometimes manifest itself in higher levels of eating disorder symptoms. Studies focused on gay and bisexual men have found a connection between higher levels of body dissatisfaction, and increased likelihood of experiencing depressive symptoms and increased sexual anxiety and poorer sexual performance.

Toni Giugliano, Policy and Public Affairs Manager at the Mental Health Foundation said: 'Millions of adults across the UK are struggling with concerns about their body image, but of all the groups surveyed, the LGBT+ community is most likely to be affected. Large numbers of LGBT+ people have said they have self-harmed or had suicidal thoughts and feelings or have felt anxious or depressed about their bodies.

'Research has shown that sexual minority men feel under pressure to feel under pressure to hold an appearance that is centred on looking slim and athletic. Pressures to live up to those ideals can have a negative impact on their emotional health.

'We found that many people identified social media as a key influence that caused them to worry about their body image. The main picture from our survey was one in which commercial, social media and advertising pressures on body image are contributing to mental health problems for millions of people.

'This social harm has been allowed to develop largely unchecked. While there have been some positive initiatives, social media companies have frequently been unwilling to take the necessary steps to protect their users from harmful content.

'That is why one of our key asks is for the UK Government to make preventing the promotion of unhealthy or idealised body image images a specific part of its forthcoming regulation strategy.'

The Foundation states that new codes of practice should include an expectation that social media companies must take practical steps to ensure that the content they promote does note exacerbate body image concerns.

The Foundation has also published an accompanying report *Body Image: How we think and feel about our bodies* which gives advice and tips on how people can take individual action to address this urgent problem.

14 May 2019

www.mentalhealth.org.uk

Encouraging children to 'socially transition' gender risks long-term harm, say NHS experts

By Henry Bodkin, health correspondent

Parents are risking psychologically damaging their children by allowing them to 'socially transition' their gender without medical or psychiatric advice, NHS experts have warned.

Primary school-aged children are increasingly being encouraged to formally switch, in defiance of the recommended 'watchful waiting' approach, the Gender Identity Development Service (GIDS) leaders said.

In some cases, children as young as six are attending school where nobody knows their original sex.

In the UK, children who display symptoms of gender dysphoria are not given hormone blockers until the onset of puberty, and cross-sex hormones may only be prescribed after they turn 16.

The GIDS psychologists, who practise at London's Tavistock Clinic, said that younger children who believe they may have been born with the wrong body should be permitted to explore behavioural aspects of the opposite gender, such as dress or types of play.

However, they warned that many such children end up preferring to remain the biological gender they were born, and that to formally socially transition before puberty risks pre-determining the outcome.

They acknowledged that well-meaning parents, faced with deeply unhappy children, can sometimes feel they have no other option.

The situation is made worse because the waiting list to see a specialist at the Tavistock and Portland Trust, the NHS's only child gender service, is now two years long.

Dr Bernadette Wren, head of clinical psychology at the trust, said: 'Social transitioning has become a really big topic.

'We have never recommended complete social transitioning but it has become a really popular thing and many advocacy groups really promote it.

'We take the long view because our concern has been that what might work to lower anxiety in a younger child may become the thing that is problematic when they get older.

'It can become harder for children as they move into adolescence, they are moving into puberty and the young person suddenly faces a wall of puberty.

'We think that is setting up problems for later.'

GIDS received 2,590 referrals in the year 2018-19, almost a four-fold increase in four years.

Earlier this year Penny Mordaunt, the equalities minister, ordered a review to establish why there has been a surge in the number of girls seeking help.

Almost three-quarters of children seeking help with their gender are now female-born.

Around 45 per cent of the children referred to the service decide to undergo physical interventions, according to GIDS.

Dr Wren said that rather than a full social transition, 'we would rather have a kind of grappling with the fact that this young person is in a slightly anomalous position but life can still be good and full of hope and there may be some solutions further down the line but it's a complicated place to be and there is no magic solution.

'For some families the social transition can work as a kind of "it's all going to be fine" and actually the system is way more complicated than that.'

The experts said various 'advocacy groups' encourage parents to opt for total social transition.

A spokesman for the Tavistock and Portman NHS Foundation Trust said: 'For some young people social transition can be very helpful. However it is important to keep things open.

'Across all contexts, including schools and local communities, we need to support young people experiencing distress around their gender identity.

'We need to support exploration, which may include a social transition for some young people. It is also important to keep curiosity about gender identity alive and be open about any young person's situation, including the reality of their physical bodies.'

Meanwhile Mermaids, a charity which supports gender-diverse children, said: 'Our approach as a charity is to take no position on the clinical or medical pathways a child or young person chooses to take.

'However, we do support the international best practice guidelines from the World Professional Association of Transgender Health, which suggest empowering people of all ages to express their gender identity freely at the present time, without pre-judging their future.

'We feel it would be far simpler and safer for the hard working and overstretched staff at the Tavistock Clinic to make such difficult decisions on such sensitive cases, if their patients were no longer forced to wait up to two years for their first appointment.'

17 July 2019

A boy in a dress is just a boy in a dress

As a trans woman I'm horrified by the pressure we're putting on children to choose their gender.

By Debbie Hayton

As a child of the 1970s, I can still recall the trauma of watching Elvis Costello jab his finger at me as he sang 'Called careers information; have you got yourself an occupation?' My dreams of becoming an astronaut had already evaporated by then and I feared I needed to make a hasty decision before I was conscripted into Oliver's Army — or worse.

A generation later, the stakes are far higher for our kids. Today the refrain might be Called social media; have you got yourself a gender identity?

It is remarkable that, although we spend so much time talking about gender identity these days, nobody can define it without recourse to either circular reasoning or sexist stereotypes — and usually both. Even legislators are guilty; the State of Massachusetts, for example, defines it as 'a person's gender-related identity, appearance or behaviour, whether or not that gender-related identity or behaviour is different from that traditionally associated with the person's physiology or assigned sex at birth'. Which doesn't exactly sound very progressive.

Layla Moran, the Lib Dem MP, may have told Parliament that she could see souls during a debate about trans issues, but all we can actually see are bodies and they have a sex rather than a gender. Which leads us to the deeper question: why do we need a gender identity?

For generations we have known about sex: there is female and there is male and we need one of each to produce the next generation.

Society devised different restrictions and expectations according to our sex, and while most people complied, some of us found them so excruciating that they crushed our mental health. That used to be called 'gender identity disorder', an identity problem relating to gender. When people objected to being labelled as 'disordered', the language was changed to gender dysphoria, but from the original terminology grew the notion of gender identity.

In itself, that is not a problem. As a transsexual I'm happy to say that I prefer to identify with females, and hence I may be described as having a female gender identity. But I am also a science teacher and, after fathering three children, two of them boys, the evidence that I was male and I am still male is overwhelming. The fact is that we have a sex and we cannot change it.

Yet with neither proof nor evidence, language has changed the way we think and many now assume that gender identity is some prescriptive innate quality that drives our personality. At a time when opinions and feelings are in the ascendency, evidence and facts are too easily jettisoned from the public consciousness as inconvenient truths. In many people's minds, gender identity has replaced biological sex as a means of dividing humanity.

Of course nobody fits perfectly into the two gender roles. There are over seven billion personalities on the planet, all unique and all a curious combination of feminine and masculine. As the theory developed, non-binary identities were created and then subdivided. At one point, Facebook suggested there were 71 different gender identities to choose from. While they have now — probably wisely — allowed users to make up their own gender identities, society loves to create boxes and then force people to identify into them.

The impact on children is massive. Have you got yourself a gender identity? The implication is that if you haven't, then you don't know yourself. BBC Education recently produced a film to help teachers counsel their pupils; there are 'over a hundred' gender identities, the primary school children were told. When I was a boy, it was traumatic enough choosing between the 92 teams in the Football League.

But unlike choosing a football team to support, or a genre of music to enjoy, the conflation of sex and gender identity places a different sort of burden on the shoulders of children, and especially those who might previously have been described as gender non-conforming: boys who like to play with dolls, or girls with more interest in football. Are they really the opposite sex? No, of course they are not. Science is clear: our sex is determined by our chromosomes, gonads and genitals. A boy who likes to wear dresses is a boy who likes to wear dresses.

But this is not the message they are hearing from society and — especially — from social media. Maybe you are transgender? Or non-binary? Or some other recently invented gender identity? With that imposed choice comes pressure, and for children approaching puberty that pressure

is unlike anything previous generations had to face. Puberty is irreversible and the clock is ticking. Children know that but they also know about puberty blockers and the possibility of delaying the onset of puberty — supposedly to buy some time.

And puberty changes the mind as well as the body. I am a teacher and I see with my own eyes the development of abstract thought that occurs in children as they go through the teenage years: delay puberty and we may be delying mental development.

Meanwhile, as their friends go through puberty, those 'buying time' are left behind. Nobody wants that, not least 14-year-old children seeing their friends developing into adults before their eyes.

The decision then has to be made: withdraw the puberty blockers and allow nature to take its course, or move to cross-sex hormones. At that stage, children still too young to be tattooed face sterilisation followed by a lifetime of medication. And the decision is theirs.

What are we thinking as a society? We do not allow 17-year-old boys to have vasectomies just because they want one. But we allow 13-year-old transgirls to elect to have treatment that leads to the same outcome: infertility before they have even reached the age of consent.

This is the context in which the polling conducted by UnHerd needs to be analysed. Few people know what is going on – they just want children to be happy in themselves. But at the same time, there is a mental health crisis among our young people, and no wonder, given the demands we place on them, including, now, the responsibility for making profound decisions about their bodies.

Life was simpler in the 1970s. If we got our profession wrong, we could re-train and have a second career; if they get their gender identity wrong the changes to their bodies may be permanent, and they cannot have a second body. Perhaps some of those children will need to transition eventually – as I did – but they need to make that decision as adults, and maybe after they have had the opportunity to have children of their own.

We should not put children in the quandary of having to decide their gender identity. It is neither progressive nor kind. Rather we should allow them true freedom – the freedom to express their personality in the sexed bodies that nature gave them.

22 November 2019

Key Facts

- Males produce sperm cells via the testes. They have an XY sex chromosome and higher levels of testosterone. (page 1)

- Females produce egg cells via the ovaries. They have an XX chromosome and higher levels of oestrogen. (page 1)

- Sometimes a person's genetic sex doesn't align with their gender identity. (page 3)

- The differences between male and female sexes are anatomical and physiological. 'Sex' tends to relate to biological differences. (page 3)

- The World Health Organization (WHO) defines gender as: 'Gender refers to the socially constructed characteristics of women and men, such as norms, roles, and relationships of and between groups of women and men. It varies from society to society and can be changed.' (page 3)

- Gender dysphoria, or gender identity disorder, is when someone is born one gender, but identifies as another. This may mean that a person born a male identifies as female, or vice versa. (page 6)

- Gender reassignment is a protected characteristic in the Equality Act 2010. (page 6)

- Sexual orientation is a term that is used to describe what gender, or genders, someone is attracted to. The most common sexual orientations that people identify with are straight, gay, lesbian, or bisexual. (page 12)

- A new YouGov survey shows more people than ever identify as somewhere between the extremes of the sexuality spectrum, with those aged 18 to 24 now eight times more likely than they were in 2015 to identify as bisexual. (page 15)

- 'Coming out' is the terminology used to describe the process of sharing your sexuality/gender identity with the world. (page 17)

- In 2019, counsellors at Childline saw 16 cases each day related to sexuality and gender issues such as bullying and suicidal thoughts, with 409 of these among 11 year-olds or younger. (page 19)

- Children's charity NSPCC saw a 40 per cent increase in young people struggling with 'coming out' to their parents between 2017-2018 and 2018-2019, and homophobic bullying was mentioned in 573 calls and emails to the service. (page 19)

- Men (2.5%) were more likely to identify as LGB than women (2.0%) in 2018. (page 20)

- An estimated 2.3% of the population aged 16 years and over (1.2 million people) identified themselves as lesbian, gay or bisexual (LGB) in 2018. (page 20)

- Legal unions for same-sex couples have only become available recently; civil partnerships were introduced for same-sex couples in the UK in December 2005, and same-sex marriage has been available in England, Wales and Scotland since 2014 and in Northern Ireland from 2020. (page 23)

- From 2014 to 2018, the proportion of people identifying as LGB who were in same-sex marriages increased from 0.8% to 7.3%, while those in civil partnerships decreased from 12.3% to 6.5%. (page 23)

- The period between 1967 and 1982 was characterized by the decriminalisation of homosexuality across the UK. (page 24)

- Same-sex activity has been legal in Denmark since 1933, and the age of consent was adopted at 15 in 1977 regardless of gender or sexual orientation. Denmark made history in 1989 when it became the first nation to offer legal recognition to same-sex partnerships with the title 'registered partnerships'. (page 24)

- Same-sex activity in Belgium was legal from as far back as 1795 with an exception for the period between 1965 and 1985. Belgium was the 2nd country in the world to legally recognize same-sex marriage in 2003. (page 24)

- In Canada, transgender individuals can change their legal gender in all territories and provinces under varying regulations. As of 2017, Canada made strides by allowing its citizens to choose a third sex, called 'X', on their Canadian passport. (page25)

- Homosexuality was decriminalised after the Russian revolution in the early 1920s. However, under Stalin, homosexuality became punishable again in 1937. It was not until 1993 that the law was repealed and homosexuality decriminalised again. (page 27)

- In May 2019 the High Court in Kenya ruled to keep the ban on gay sex, which is punishable by 14 years in jail. The National Gay & Lesbian Human Rights Commission disagree and are appealing the judgement. (page 28)

- The rate of LGBT hate crime per capita rose by 144% between 2013-14 and 2017-18. In the most recent year of data, police recorded 11,600 crimes, more than doubling from 4,600 during this period. (page 30)

- Stonewall surveyed 3,713 young people aged 11 to 19 across Britain, from November 2016 to February 2017. The survey was for young people who are lesbian, gay, bi or trans, or who think they might be. 16% of those surveyed reported themselves to be trans. (page 34)

- Approximately one in 25 people aged between 16 and 24 in the UK identify as lesbian, gay or bisexual, according to the Office for National Statistics. (page 35)

- One third (33 per cent) of the LGBT+ community said they had experienced suicidal thoughts and feelings in relation to their body image. (page 36)

- GIDS (Gender Identity Development Service) received 2,590 referrals in the year 2018-19, almost a four-fold increase in four years. (page 37)

Asexual/asexuality

A person who has no (or very low) sexual feelings, desires or attraction to anyone. However, just because someone isn't sexually attracted to anyone does not mean they cannot be romantically attracted to others (e.g. seeking a relationship for love and companionship that isn't sexual).

Bisexual

Someone who defines themselves as bisexual or 'bi' is attracted to people of either sex. While a bisexual person may be equally attracted to men and women, this does not have to be the case: they may feel a stronger attraction to one sex than the other, or feel attraction to different sexes at different points in their lives.

Coming out

'Coming out' happens when an LGB person feels ready to tell their friends and family about their sexual orientation. As heterosexuality is the most common sexual orientation, those close to them will probably have assumed they were straight. Coming out is a big step for most gay people, especially if they fear a negative reaction from some people. It is quite common for gay people to not be fully 'out', and only let certain people know about their sexuality.

Gender

Gender is sexual identity, especially in relation to society or culture; the condition of being female or male. Gender refers to socially-constructed roles, learned behaviours and expectations associated with females and males. Gender is more than just biology: it is the understanding we gain from society and those around us of what it means to be a girl/woman or a boy/man.

Gender dysphoria

Sometimes known as a gender identity disorder or transgenderism, gender dysphoria is a where a person feels strongly that there is a mismatch between their biological sex (their body) and gender identity (their emotional and psychological identity) – a person may experience distress or discomfort as they feel they are "trapped" inside a body that doesn't match their gender identity. Gender dysphoria is a recognised medical condition, for which treatment is sometimes appropriate (for some people this means dressing and living as their preferred gender, for others it can mean taking hormones or having surgery to change their physical appearance). It's not a mental illness.

Gender identity

The gender that a person 'identifies' with, or feels themselves to be. This is not always the same as their sex recorded at birth.

Hate Crime

Hate Crime is criminal behaviour where the perpetrator is motivated by hostility or demonstrates hostility towards the victim's disability, race, religion, sexual orientation or transgender identity. These things are 'protected characteristics'. A hate crime can include verbal abuse, intimidation, threats, harassment, assault and bullying, as well as damage to property.

Heterosexual

Someone who is attracted exclusively to people of the opposite sex to themselves. Heterosexuality is the most common sexual orientation. It is often referred to as 'straight', although some people feel that this is not the best term to use and has the potential to be offensive – it may imply negative connotations for other sexual orientations which may then be seen as 'crooked' in contrast and therefore negative.

Homophobia

Homophobia is the irrational fear or hatred of homosexuality (an aversion towards lesbian, gay or bisexual people). This fear can lead to behaviour that discriminates against LGBT people and consequently advantages heterosexuals. Such discrimination is illegal under the Equality Act (Sexual Orientation) Regulations 2007.

Homosexual

Someone who defines themselves as homosexual is attracted exclusively to people of the same sex as themselves. People of this sexual orientation may prefer to call themselves gay, or a lesbian if they are female. While some gay people may use other words such as 'queer' or 'dyke' to describe themselves, these are not considered universally acceptable and other gay people may find them offensive.

LGBT/LGBTI/LGBTQ+

LGBT stands for 'lesbian, gay, bisexual and transgender', and is often used as a shorthand way of referring to sexual orientations other than heterosexual. As language and terminology evolve, there are now several other variations of this acronym: the I refers to intersex; Q stands for queer; and the + represents asexual, pansexual, transsexual, intersex, questioning and intergender.

Non-binary

If someone is non-binary this means that they do not exclusively identify as one gender. This can be a person who: identifies as both masculine and feminine (androgynous); identifies between male and female (intergender); or as neutral or don't identify with a gender (agender).

Sexual orientation

Sexual orientation refers to a person's physical, romantic and/or emotional attraction towards other people. Sexual orientation is usually defined either as heterosexual or 'straight' (attraction to the opposite sex); homosexual or 'gay'/'lesbian' (attraction to the same sex); or bisexual (attraction to both sexes).

Sexuality

The word 'sexuality' is often used interchangeably with 'sexual orientation' in debates concerning LGBT issues. However, it actually has a wider meaning, referring to human sexual behaviour in general.

Transgender

A transgender person is someone who identifies as the opposite gender than that into which they were born, and who has chosen to live their life in that gender. They may or may not have gone through gender reassignment surgery. Someone's gender identity is separate from their sexual orientation: however, issues concerning transgender people and their rights tend to be discussed in relation to debates about sexuality, as they often suffer similar kinds of discrimination to LGB people. These issues do also cross over into debates concerning equal gender rights, however.

Transphobia

Transphobia is the irrational fear or hatred of transpeople. This fear can lead to behaviour that discriminates against LGBT people and consequently advantages heterosexuals. Such discrimination is illegal under the Equality Act (Sexual Orientation) Regulations 2007.

Activities

Brainstorming

◆ In small groups, discuss what you know about sexuality and gender. Consider the following points:

  · What is sexuality?

  · What is gender identity?

  · What is the difference between gender and sex?

◆ In pairs, write a list of gender stereotypes. Do you believe these to be true? If not, then why?

Research

◆ What stereotypes exist surrounding gay men, lesbian women and transgender people? Can you think of any films or television programmes you watch, or books you have read, which perpetrate these stereotypes? Can you think of any which challenge them? Make some notes and discuss with a partner.

◆ Choose an LGBT person from history, or an influential figure from today, and write a fact file about them.

◆ Research 'coming out' stories and write some tips for a person who has decided to come out to their friends and family.

◆ Create a questionnaire to find out if your classmates have experienced or witnessed any homophobic or transphobic bullying. Present your findings in an infographic.

◆ Research key events in LGBT+ history and create a timeline.

◆ Choose a country and look into the laws they have regarding LGBT+ issues. Compare them to the laws we have in the UK. Are they better or worse? Read *The 10 best countries for LGBT rights* for some inspiration.

◆ Read *Faith and LGBT inclusion* and choose two different religions. Research their attitudes to LGBT+ issues and compare and contrast the two.

Design

◆ Design a poster with 'ground rules' when discussing LGBT+ issues.

◆ In small groups create a signposting poster, with organisations that support young LGBT people.

◆ Create your own slogan to help tackle homophobic, biphobic & transphobic bullying and incorporate it into a poster which could be displayed your schools.

◆ Create a leaflet for teens who are questioning their sexual orientation. You might want to explore different LGBT+ terms, as well as including links and phone numbers to resources they might find helpful.

◆ Choose one of the articles in this topic and create an illustration to highlight its key themes/message.

Oral

◆ Coming out to parents can be a challenging time for gay and lesbian young people. In pairs, role-play a scenario in which a young person tells their parents about their sexual orientation for the first time. Imagine the feelings of both parties during your conversation.

◆ 'Age-appropriate, LGBT-inclusive sex and relationship education should be compulsory in schools.' Discuss this statement in groups and feed back to the class.

◆ In small groups discuss homophobic, biphobic & transphobic bullying and how you can prevent it from happening.

◆ In pairs, discuss gender and what you understand about it. Consider stereotypes and how they affect children.

◆ In small groups, discuss why you think that a larger proportion of LGBT+ people have problems with their body image. Read *'Worryingly high' levels of body image anxiety in the LGBT+ community revealed in new Mental Health Foundation poll* for information.

Reading/writing

◆ Write a one-paragraph definition of nonbinary.

◆ Read the article *Childline receives 6,000 calls from young people struggling with sexuality and gender identity* and then imagine you are the child in the article. Write a letter to explain to your parents why you feel you are trans, and how their behaviour towards you affects you.

◆ Choose one of the articles in this book and write a short summary. Pick out five key facts and include them.

◆ Read *Boys Don't Cry* by Malorie Blackman. Write a book review.

◆ Watch *She's the Man* (2006), and consider the gender roles in the film. How does this compare to Shakespeare's *Twelfth Night*?

◆ Watch *The Imitation Game* (2014), and write a short review. Consider the changes in law since World War II and the effect that Alan Turing had on these changes.

◆ Write a diary entry of a young person who is questioning their sexuality. Consider how their family might respond, will they be positive or negative?

Acknowledgements

The publisher is grateful for permission to reproduce the material in this book. While every care has been taken to trace and acknowledge copyright, the publisher tenders its apology for any accidental infringement or where copyright has proved untraceable. The publisher would be pleased to come to a suitable arrangement in any such case with the rightful owner.

The material reproduced in ISSUES books is provided as an educational resource only. The views, opinions and information contained within reprinted material in ISSUES books do not necessarily represent those of Independence Educational Publishers and its employees.

Images

Cover image courtesy of iStock. All other images courtesy of Pixabay and Unsplash, except pages 3, 5, 8, 16, 29, 33, 36, & 39: Freepik

Illustrations

Don Hatcher: pages 10 & 17. Simon Kneebone: pages 14 & 25. Angelo Madrid: pages 7 & 22.

Additional acknowledgements

With thanks to the Independence team: Shelley Baldry, Danielle Lobban, Jackie Staines and Jan Sunderland.

Tracy Biram

Cambridge, May 2020